PRAISE FOR

Color-Courageous Discipleship Student Edition

"Young people's passion for racial justice can lead us all forward—but they need deep discipleship like this book. I want the diverse teenagers you and I care about most to be trained by Michelle. Her fresh scriptural insights and practical ideas will help this generation be on mission with Jesus and courageously bring healing to our world."

—KARA POWELL, PhD, executive director of Fuller Youth Institute
and co-author of *3 Big Questions That Change Every Teenager*

"I highly recommend this book to all youth workers navigating difficult conversations with their youth around the racial tensions and injustices in our world. From her own lived experience, Michelle does an amazing job of walking us through our own racial awakening by educating, enlightening, and encouraging us with spiritual practices and practical tools that help us engage in color-courageous discipleship."

—ROBERT ABOITES, COO of Urban Youth Workers Institute

"Diverse young people long to live an embodied faith, and *Color-Courageous Discipleship Student Edition* teaches them how! An invitation to adventure in understanding their unique identity and impact on the world through historical patterns, present-day injustice, and the real Jesus's command to make disciples of all cultures and ethnicities, this book is what every teenager today needs to pursue antiracism for Jesus and help build beloved community."

—YULEE LEE, PhD, senior director of staff culture and diversity,
equity, and inclusion at Fuller Youth Institute

"The future is young, urban, and multiethnic. If we want to participate in what God is doing in his church, these are essential conversations we need to have. Michelle beautifully guides us in how to integrate a more holistic gospel to reach this next generation with and for Christ."

—TOMMY NIXON, CEO of Urban Youth Workers Institute

"Michelle Sanchez helps us look at our own color-courageous journey by first being profoundly honest about her own discipleship journey. Her discussion questions are excellent. And I love her definition of discipleship."

—REV. DOUG SCHAUPP, national director of evangelism for InterVarsity Christian Fellowship

"Understanding issues of race in our current cultural context can feel so challenging. Even in the church, this is a conversation that many times feels scary and difficult. What we all need—students, parents, and church leaders alike—is someone wise and compassionate to lead us through the stickiness of it all. Michelle Sanchez draws from Scripture and from her own extensive experiences to provide us with a biblical, practical way forward. By working through *Color-Courageous Discipleship Student Edition,* you can gain a deeper understanding about issues of race and move from a posture of fear and avoidance to one of courage and engagement."

—HELEN LEE, author and speaker

COLOR-COURAGEOUS DISCIPLESHIP STUDENT EDITION

COLOR-COURAGEOUS DISCIPLESHIP

STUDENT EDITION

FOLLOW JESUS, DISMANTLE RACISM, AND
BUILD BELOVED COMMUNITY

MICHELLE T. SANCHEZ

WATERBROOK

For P.J.,
with gratitude for the impact
of your ministry to youth.

Have I not commanded you? Be strong and courageous.
Do not be afraid; do not be discouraged, for the LORD
your God will be with you wherever you go.

—JOSHUA 1:9

CONTENTS

PART 3

COLOR-COURAGEOUS SPIRITUAL PRACTICES 133

PART ONE

INTRODUCTION TO COLOR-COURAGEOUS DISCIPLESHIP

INVITATION TO A RACIAL DISCIPLESHIP JOURNEY

You may be wondering, *What does race have to do with disciple-ship?* Great question! Although I am both African American and a national discipleship leader, I am still baffled by this question. For much of my life, I have not made concrete connections between race and discipleship. Does that matter?

I mean, it's pretty obvious that followers of Jesus shouldn't be racist bullies, right? Personally, I am *for* Jesus as well as all races of people. I am *against* all forms of racism, full stop. I bet most people reading this, including you, would agree. So . . . aren't we good? What more is there to talk about? Racism can be such a depressing topic. I'd much rather talk about Jesus!

But see, that's the problem: *Race* and *discipleship* aren't completely separate things, like apples and clementines. Actually, they are related in pretty eye-popping ways! What's more, I now realize this exciting truth: One of the best ways for this generation to grow as disciples of Jesus is to understand what race is all about and, together with Jesus, to resist racism as color-courageous disciples.

What makes a disciple "color-courageous"? Color-courageous disciples understand that it *isn't* so helpful to be "color-blind," moving through life as though race doesn't exist and doesn't matter. I *wish* race didn't matter too! But as we will soon discover, it does. In fact, racism continues to cause untold suffering throughout the world and in the lives of people whom Jesus loves. But disciples of Jesus are not powerless—we can make a difference.

The great news is that as disciples we can become part of the solution as we move from color-blind to color-courageous. Not only that, but we can get to know Jesus better on the way.

Finally, I'm starting to get it. By missing the connection between race and discipleship, I've been missing out on experiencing more of Jesus as a color-courageous disciple! I promise to share more of my story with you—but, ultimately, this is about *your* story. Even now, as you are reading, you are opening your personal invitation to a brand-new discipleship adventure. In fact, that's why I wrote this book: I don't want you—or any other disciple—to miss out on all that Jesus has for you.

DISCIPLESHIP DEFINED

I know we've already been talking about *disciples* and *discipleship,* but before we continue on our journey, let's make sure we're clear on what discipleship is. My favorite definition for **discipleship** comes from Jesus's invitation to his first disciples: "Follow Me, and I will make you fishers of people" (Matthew 4:19, NASB). From this brief but brilliant invitation, we discover three elements of discipleship: A disciple (1) *follows Jesus,* (2) *is transformed by Jesus,* and (3) *is on mission with Jesus.*

First, a disciple *follows Jesus.* A disciple's life isn't centered on religious stuff but on the person of Jesus Christ. A disciple has accepted Jesus Christ as Savior (our rescuer) and Lord (our leader). (By the way, if you are not yet a disciple of Jesus or want to learn more about what that means, don't miss my special invitation for "not-yet-followers" of Jesus at the back of this book!)

Second, a disciple is *being transformed by Jesus*. This means that Jesus constantly shapes his disciples to be more like him. Finally, a disciple is *on mission with Jesus*. In other words, disciples partner with Jesus to heal the world . . . and make more disciples!

MATTHEW 4:19	
A disciple . . .	
Follow Me,	Follows Jesus . . .
and I will make you	is transformed by Jesus . . .
fishers of people.	is on mission with Jesus.

SO, WHAT IS *RACIAL DISCIPLESHIP*?

Racial discipleship, like all discipleship, involves all three discipleship dimensions. It is about following Jesus more closely as we encounter racial challenges, being transformed by Jesus in our racial mindsets and interactions, and embarking on mission with Jesus as we partner with him to bring racial healing to the world. As we strive for all three, we will pursue antiracism not as some fashionable trend but as an ongoing expression of our discipleship—which is exactly what it should be.

And now we must ponder a surprising idea: *You have already been racially discipled.* Whether you realize it or not, you have already been set up by the world to engage with race in certain ways. We have all been subtly influenced by the culture, practices, and perspectives of the family we were raised in, the place we grew up in, and even the era that we find ourselves in. The question is not *if* you have been racially discipled. The question is *how.*

That is why what many disciples need now is to embark on a different kind of racial discipleship journey—different, in that this time it will be intentional. Different, in that this time we will orient ourselves as disciples of Jesus Christ to engage effectively with the racial challenges we face, in Jesus's name. When it comes to race, most of us need to be intentionally "rediscipled."[1] That is, we need to be discipled *again*. What's more, on this journey we will discover that racial discipleship is not just about resisting racism or transforming the world. It is certainly that, but it is far more: *Racial discipleship is about being personally transformed so that you can experience more of Jesus.* And *that* is what has been the most exciting part of the journey for me.

**You can make a profound difference for Jesus—
perhaps especially because you are young.**

By the way, yes, this invitation is for *you*—whatever your race might be. None of us have a perfect perspective when it comes to race. That includes me. I can't tell you how surprised I was when I came to understand that I had been doing things to perpetuate racism too! When it comes to race, we *all* need awakening, transformation, healing, and a fresh vision to forge a better future together. Although our individual racial discipleship journeys will have different starting points and milestones, I believe that the journey itself is universal.

And yes, this invitation is also for you, whatever your *age* might be. In fact, God calls young disciples to be examples for older ones. And that's not *my* idea. It's from the Bible: "Don't let anyone look down on you because you are young, but set an example for the believers in speech, in conduct, in love, in faith and in purity" (1 Timothy 4:12). No matter what anyone says, you can make a profound difference for Jesus—perhaps *especially* because you are young.

As disciples of Christ, we are *all* invited to awaken to the racial brokenness of the world: young and old, male and female,

Black and White—and beyond. And we are all invited to come up with solutions for our future together.

It's not enough to avoid *racism—to make a difference, we must learn how to* resist *racism.*

As far as solutions go, here's the crux of the matter: It's no longer enough for you to say, "I'm not racist." It's no longer enough to merely be a *nonracist* disciple. If you really want to make a difference and reflect God's heart, you must become an *antiracist* disciple. That means you must learn not only how to *avoid* racism—more importantly, you must learn how to actively *resist* racism as a color-courageous disciple. Together, we will discover how.

NOW IS THE RIGHT TIME TO DO *SOMETHING*

Your generation has been witness to a profound racial reckoning that has swept the world—with the devastating death of George Floyd in 2020 as a pivotal moment. Many have asked new questions and taken new steps to learn and grow. People of all ages, ethnic backgrounds, and faith traditions are wondering about racism again and asking, "What can I do?" Yet as Christians, we must also ask additional, deeper questions in light of our primary commitment to Jesus Christ: "Jesus, what are you inviting me, as your *disciple,* to do? And how can I grow closer to you in the process?" In this book, we will explore these questions.

But before diving in, let's have a brief vocabulary lesson. I think that people get stuck in conversations about race because, although they use the *same words,* they use them in very *different ways,* so then everyone ends up confused! Let's try to avoid that on our journey, shall we?

THE GEORGE FLOYD PROTESTS

George Perry Floyd, Jr., (October 14, 1973—May 25, 2020) was an African American man who was killed by a police officer during an arrest in Minneapolis, Minnesota. Floyd was arrested because he was suspected of using a fake twenty-dollar bill to buy something at a store. Floyd grew up in Houston and played football and basketball in high school and college. He also served as a mentor in his religious community. Derek Chauvin, one of four police officers who were at the scene, subdued Floyd by kneeling on his neck and back for nine minutes and twenty-nine seconds. As Floyd slowly died of suffocation, he repeatedly said, "I can't breathe." After Floyd's death, protests against police brutality—especially toward Black people—quickly spread across the United States and around the world. In fact, polls in summer 2020 estimated that between fifteen and twenty-six million people had participated at some point in the demonstrations in the United States, making the protests the largest in U.S. history. Nearly one year later, on April 20, 2021, Chauvin was found guilty of murder and manslaughter. Like everyone else, Floyd was not perfect. And it is true that at times he even got into trouble with the law. Nevertheless, George Floyd was created in the image of God. He did not deserve to die in this way. All people deserve to be treated with dignity.

Mural portrait of George Floyd by Eme Street Art in Mauerpark (Berlin, Germany)

RACE VS. ETHNICITY—WHAT'S THE DIFFERENCE?

Race and *ethnicity* are not the same thing. From a biblical perspective, there is a big difference between race and ethnicity, and it is helpful for disciples to understand that difference.

I once attended a conference where an African American speaker said, "God did not create race. In the beginning, there was no race." At the time, I was shocked. What was he talking about? Of course God created race! He loves race! Well, over time I have come to the surprising realization that the presenter was right. What God created—what God delights in—is not *race* but *ethnicity*. Let's get clear on the difference by beginning at the end.

———

One day, not so far from today, you will open your eyes in heaven. However you arrived—whether by an abrupt accident, a long and painful illness, or a soft final sigh—will be a fuzzy memory. In a flash, your former life will be a dream. You are now fully and deliciously awake.

You greedily gulp the air—heavy, fresh, and sweet—as your unfamiliar eyes adjust to the light—if this golden, flowing joy can be called light. This light is not thin and fleeting like the light you knew on earth. No, this radiance is pure, pulsing, weighty. *Light* is too small a word. You are bathed in glory.

What's more, the *prism* of this glory defies description. You are awash in color—and what colors these are! Brilliant colors you have never seen, sparking new emotions you have never felt.

This glory also glimmers . . . with personality. It welcomes you, floods your heart, embraces your soul, rejoices over every no-longer-hidden part of you. Love, sheer love, unobstructed love, crazy love! Now you understand. Paradise is not a place. It is a *presence.* Paradise is love, the very presence of God. Sweet relief—God is here. God is with you in this place, closer than your own self, rapturously real. You will never be afraid again.

You become aware of the gentle trickle of a stream. When you look, you see not a stream but a river of pure crystal. It seems alive. You begin to follow the river and the glory toward their source—a cascading garden city. And you can tell there is a party going on!

You are joined by countless saints of every color, every hue, every imaginable variety. Together you walk down transparent streets of gold toward the city's center. Without being told, you know: These are your friends; this is your family. And only together with them do you see it: love itself—God—sitting on a throne, resplendent in rainbow. You erupt with the symphony of saints in worship, captivated by the sheer rainbowness of it all—this gorgeous rainbow God, surrounded by a rainbow throne, worshipped wildly by rainbow people from every tribe, nation, people, language, and culture. And it is in this prismatic moment that you finally behold something you have been waiting your whole life to see: the forever smile of God.

In this depiction of the new creation, the Bible paints us a beautiful picture of **shalom,** the Hebrew word that means "how things are *supposed* to be." Shalom is what we experience whenever and wherever the kingdom of God comes true. Although the word is sometimes translated as "peace," biblical shalom is so much more. Shalom is wholeness and flourishing in every dimension of creation, including ethnicity.

SHALOM

Here is what the word *shalom* looks like in Hebrew:

שלום

Did you ever get the sense that the world is not as it should be? Your intuition is right—you were created for something far better. You were created for shalom. *Shalom* is a Hebrew word from the Bible that is usually translated as "peace"—yet its meaning is far richer than the English word *peace*. *Shalom* essentially means "the world as it should be"—a world marked by abundance, perfection, flourishing, and joy. At its heart, *shalom* signifies a web of *right relationships*—especially between people and God, between peoples of different ethnicities, and between people and all of creation. Color-courageous discipleship narrows in on what disciples can do to restore shalom between people of different racial and ethnic groups. Dr. Martin Luther King, Jr., called this type of shalom "beloved community." Of course, we cannot expect to experience perfect shalom now. Only when Jesus returns will the Lord "wipe every tear" from our eyes in a world that contains "'no more death' or mourning or crying or pain" (Revelation 21:4). However, in the meantime, we *can* work to experience a foretaste of God's shalom in our churches and other communities—through the power of the Holy Spirit that God has given us.

The book of Revelation portrays how history will climax in a new creation where people from every nation that ever existed will gather to worship God: "After this I looked, and there before me was a great multitude that no one could count, from every nation, tribe, people and language, standing before the throne and before the Lamb" (Revelation 7:9).

But let's take a magnifying glass to the word translated here as "nation." When you hear the word *nation,* I bet you think of a country—a place like Nigeria, Spain, or Brazil. However, the Greek word here is *ethne.* It's where our contemporary word *ethnicity* comes from. We are called to make disciples not only of far-flung nations, but also of diverse ethnic groups, right where we are. Around God's throne there will be people not just from every nation, but also from every *ethnicity* within nations. Know what that means? History will climax in a multiethnic party!

This is our definition of **ethnicity,** and we will also explore each phrase:

> **Ethnicity is a God-ordained cultural identity that God delights in as a means of bringing glory to himself and enrichment to his kingdom.**

First, ethnicity is *God-ordained.* Scripture displays God's passionate intention for diversity from beginning to end, including ethnic diversity. We see it in so many places: in the teeming diversity of God's creation, in the temple that God commanded Israel to build for all nations, in the Savior who came to be a light for all peoples, and in the fiery, multicolored birth of the church on **Pentecost**—just to name a few. God both created and delights in ethnic diversity.

Second, *ethnic diversity brings greater glory to God.* How? Here's one way: Though humans were created in the image of God, no one individual, ethnicity, or culture can reflect the fullness of who God is. Diverse ethnicities and cultures, in fellowship together, best reflect the unimaginably diverse aspects of God.

Finally, *ethnic diversity enriches God's kingdom.* One of my favorite scriptures about the new creation shows all the ethnic peoples of the world streaming into the garden city of God with their unique cultural treasures and contributions (see Revelation 21:26; Isaiah 60:11). As a connoisseur of multicultural cuisine, I certainly hope those treasures include food. Who knows what delights we may savor in the new creation? Perhaps not only a feast of Vietnamese pho, Ethiopian injera, and French ratatouille but also New Orleans gumbo, Minnesota wild rice, and Southern fried chicken!

Ethnic diversity—fully redeemed in all its beauty and its brilliance—will be one aspect of the new creation that will make it fascinating and fulfilling beyond anything we have imagined.

You may have noticed that I did not mention the word *race* in the previous Bible discussion. That is because race is not a biblical concept. *Other than the concept of the "human race," you will find no mention of race in the Bible as we understand it today.* That came as a surprise to me too!

> **Other than the concept of the "human race," you will find no mention of race in the Bible.**

But what do we mean by **race**? Here is our definition:

Race is a man-made system that divides humans into categories based on visible traits like skin color. These categories are usually established so that one racial group might gain power over another group.

People used to identify more with *ethnicity*. *Race* is a relatively new concept that emerged in past centuries as Europeans sought to justify the colonization of non-Europeans. **Colonialism** is what happens when powerful countries seek to control less powerful countries, often becoming even more powerful as a result.

European colonialists needed a simple excuse to demean people and steal their land. So, they created this system called "race" as a solution—and it was an effective one.

Here's an example of how it happened. One contributor to the creation of racial divisions was Carl Linnaeus, the eighteenth-century Swedish botanist commonly known as the father of modern taxonomy. Taxonomy is the scientific process of classifying or putting things into different categories. We're still influenced by Linnaeus today in science class whenever we refer to the concepts of species, genus, and family—these were his ideas. Like an excitable kid arranging his blocks, Linnaeus clearly got a kick out of organizing things. Unfortunately, he also started to categorize *people* along with beasts!

Linnaeus came to delineate racial categories based primarily on skin color. These skin colors included *Europaeus* (white), *Americanus* (reddish), *Asiaticus* (dark), and *Africanus* (black).[2] Clearly, though, these racial categories emerged from a racist perspective. You see, Linnaeus did not stop at creating racial categories; he also ordered those races into hierarchies—meaning that he put some races at the top and others at the bottom. Of course, he always ensured that his own race was at the top! Carl Linnaeus is just one unfortunate example of a slew of powerful people who organized both humans *and* beasts into hierarchies.

Linnaeus's Skin Color Hierarchy

Europaeus
(White)

Americanus
(Reddish)

Asiaticus
(Dark)

Africanus
(Black)

So, we can now clearly understand the difference between *ethnicity* and *race:* Ethnicity was God's idea; race was our idea. Ethnicity is natural; race is artificial. Ethnicity will endure forever; humanity's racial divisions will cease when God's new creation comes.

ETHNICITY	RACE
God's idea	Our idea
Natural	Artificial
Eternal	Temporary

FROM RACISM TO ANTIRACISM

Now we turn to the definition of *racism*. We can't resist racism if we don't really understand racism. And guess what? It's not as obvious as you think! **Racism** is personal racial prejudice *plus* systemic practices by institutions that lead to racial inequity in society. Or to say it in a simpler way:

Racism = Personal Prejudice + Systemic Inequity

There's a lot packed into that description, so let's take a closer look. **Prejudice** comes from two word parts meaning "before" (*pre-*) and "judge" (*-judice*). So if you are racially *prejudiced,* it means that when it comes to race, you "judge before." You make preconceived judgments about people—both positive and negative—based on race. And here's the thing. *You may not even be aware that you're doing it.* Personal prejudice can be both conscious and unconscious. That's one reason that racism continues to plague our world today. And then, unfortunately, personal prejudice all too easily leads to discrimination. **Discrimination** is the act of treating people from different racial groups differently, typically with some groups receiving better treatment than others.

As it turns out, we all exhibit unconscious biases in different ways throughout life—even as early as three years old! In one study, preschoolers were shown to use racial categories during playtime to identify, exclude, and even negotiate power with other kids.[3] And, as you might imagine, the problem tends to get worse as we get older—not better. Whether we realize it or not, adults still aren't playing fair when it comes to race.

The second part of our definition of racism is "systemic practices by institutions that lead to racial inequity in society." When something is **systemic,** it means that it doesn't just impact *individual people* but also *entire systems.* More and more people are beginning to understand that racism has both personal and systemic dimensions. If you think about it, that shouldn't be a surprise. After all, our systems and institutions were created by and continue to be run by *people*—the very same people who have those racial biases we just talked about! We are reminded that it's not only humans—but also *systems created by humans*—that are defective. When we refer to **systemic racism,** what we mean is that patterns of racial inequity characterize many of our systems, policies, and institutions as a whole. I am thinking in particular of systems like our criminal justice system, our healthcare system, and our educational system. Many of these systems can be identified as "racist" not because they are somehow intentionally mean to people of color, but simply because their practices consistently result in unequal racial outcomes. For example, it was recently reported that U.S. minority-White school districts received $23 billion less in funding than majority-White school districts.[4] Not fair, right? We are going to explore many more examples of systemic racism, but let's be clear from the get-go: The problem has reached epidemic proportions.

Unfortunately, although race is not a biblical concept, the

construct of race is here to stay for the foreseeable future. Race still matters in that in makes a real difference in people's lives. That is why it no longer works for us to have a color-blind approach to race. What we need now is to move from color-blind to color-courageous. And we need color-courageous disciples to intentionally counteract racism with *anti*-racism.

What is antiracism? **Antiracism** is essentially racism's opposite: *the practice of becoming aware of and uprooting personal racial prejudice **plus** working to dismantle systemic practices that lead to racial inequity.* Or, to put it simply:

Antiracism = Uprooting Personal Prejudice + Dismantling Systemic Inequity

You might, perhaps, find this definition of antiracism to be overwhelming. After hundreds of years of racism, can you really make a meaningful dent now? What's more, can ordinary people—including ordinary *young* people like you—really do much to dismantle systemic racism?

The beautiful answer is yes! Because here's the thing: Even if you can't change *the* world (as a whole), you can certainly change *your* world. And if we all did just that, imagine the difference it would make!

Some have raised an important objection to the word *antiracism*. Some have said to me, "I don't really want to be 'anti-' anything! That sounds so negative." Another person said, "One of the challenges with the word *antiracism* is that it makes clear what you're against but not what you are for." These are good points.

When it comes to the racism conversation, I must admit that there are no perfect words. Rather than the word *antiracism,* some prefer phrases like *racial righteousness* and *racial reconciliation.* Yet these phrases have their shortcomings too. For me, the word *antiracism* has been most personally transformational—that's why

I'm sharing it with you. The word *antiracism* has made crystal clear to me that being "nonracist" is not enough, that being "neutral" in matters of race is not sufficient. Racism is a pernicious problem. It's still here after hundreds of years, and it won't go away anytime soon unless we all start doing something very different. When it comes to defeating racism, the word *antiracism* clarifies for me that I need to dismantle racism *proactively* and *intentionally* if I hope to make a real and lasting difference.

With all that being said, my favorite new and creative phrase when it comes to a Christian approach to antiracism is *color-courageous discipleship*. Implied in the term itself is a positive, proactive call for disciples to courageously resist racism in Jesus's name. So, color-courageous disciples are against racism, but what are they for? What is our end goal?

For me, the culmination of color-courageous discipleship is the creation of beloved community—one that is grounded in Christlike, agape love for God and for one another amid all our differences. So now we come to our guiding definition for color-courageous discipleship:

Color-courageous discipleship is the courageous, lifelong journey of following Jesus, dismantling racism, and building beloved community.

A beloved community is a community grounded in Christlike love for God and for one another amid all our differences. Love is always the disciple's goal, and it's a goal worth giving our lives for.

INVITATION TO A NEW DISCIPLESHIP ADVENTURE

Did you know that following Jesus does not mean responding just one time to his invitation? After you say yes to Jesus for the first time, he will have *many* more discipleship invitations for you during your lifetime. And each one is an invitation to a new adventure. Consider this book to be your invitation to the adventure of racial discipleship!

By the way, I love the definition of *adventure:* An adventure is a journey that is both *exciting* and *hazardous.*[5] The discipleship adventure is *exciting* because it gives you a new opportunity to know Christ better and partner with him to see God's dreams come true. But it is also *hazardous* because it requires you to risk loss and pain along the way. Like every discipleship journey, the journey of racial discipleship will require you to carry your cross, take risks, and possibly experience loss and pain. As Jesus said, "Whoever wants to be my disciple must deny themselves and take up their cross daily and follow me" (Luke 9:23). In other words, every true discipleship adventure requires courage.

As disciples of Christ, our call to courage is simultaneously a call to the cross. I have no idea what your unique cross may entail on the journey of racial discipleship, but God may invite you to

- enter into repentance, confession, and forgiveness
- engage in conversations that produce discomfort, anger, or disagreement
- uncover unconscious biases that have caused harm
- revisit painful moments
- acknowledge the shortcomings of the church or other organizations you love
- experience suspicion or rejection by others
- sacrifice in unfamiliar ways as you courageously love God and others

Yet, at the same time, let's also remember that discipleship never ends with the cross. It ends with resurrection! On the other side of the cross, there is always new life. What that resurrection life will entail for you on this journey is God's surprise, but perhaps you may

- see more of the world and its people from God's perspective
- understand the gospel more deeply, in the depths of both your brokenness and God's grace
- awaken to life-changing insights from the racial and ethnic journeys of others
- enjoy new friendships and richer, more authentic community
- know deeper levels of liberation from fear, sin, and shame
- discover God's presence and experience God in new ways
- experience healing or help others heal
- become more effective at bringing shalom and beloved community to your world
- celebrate when new disciples of Christ are made

At times, color-courageous discipleship will feel difficult, dangerous, or both—which is precisely why you need Jesus as your leader and the Bible as your anchor. You need supernatural courage for this journey. Courage is the "mental or moral strength to venture, persevere, and withstand danger, fear, or difficulty."[6] Only in Christ will we find the power, wisdom, and grace we need to flourish as color-courageous disciples.

AN OVERVIEW OF THE JOURNEY

Our racial discipleship journey will have three main parts. This is part 1, your invitation to pursue a racial discipleship journey grounded in Jesus Christ.

Part 2 will explore four color-courageous discipleship paradigm shifts. These paradigm shifts will empower you not only to grow in antiracism but also to experience Jesus in new ways as you do so.

Part 3 will investigate the place of spiritual practices (also known as spiritual disciplines) in the life of color-courageous disciples. We will revisit spiritual practices because racism is, at its core, a spiritual problem—and it requires spiritual solutions. Without spiritual practices, we are left to pursue antiracism with our own strength alone. Not a good idea! But *with* spiritual practices, our pursuit of antiracism can become an intimate journey with Jesus Christ. Spiritual practices allow us to access God's strength. What's more, spiritual practices empower us to be transformed as we transform the world.

Our journey will be grounded in God's Word. But based on our discussion so far, I also want to clarify one thing: It would be incorrect to say that the Bible *directly* engages race. The Bible does not condemn racism, and it does not encourage antiracism—*because race wasn't invented yet!* Nevertheless, the Bible *does* portray plenty of conflict between diverse groups, including diverse ethnic groups. For example, we do find **ethnocentrism** in the Bible—the far more ancient belief that one's ethnic group is central and/or superior to others. With that said, I believe there is much we can learn about race and racism from the Bible by virtue of how the Bible engages ethnicity, ethnocentrism, and related challenges.

A FEW WORDS ABOUT WORDS

Becoming a color-courageous disciple involves seeing the world in some new ways. To see the world in new ways, it helps to have new words. That is why I have included in the appendix an extensive glossary for you. Don't tell anyone, but when I was a kid, I read the dictionary for fun. Yes, I'm aware that makes me weird! With that said, you can be sure that reading the glossary alone would be a spectacular way to expand your horizons. Throughout this book, you will find glossary words in bold text.

When I refer to people, I will use the following terms interchangeably: **people of color** and **minority,** as well as **White** and **majority.** I do get that these words aren't perfect either. For example, the terms *minority* and *majority* are waning in usage because they are becoming outdated: The census predicts that by 2045, if not sooner, the United States is projected to be "minority White."

I will use *people of color* to refer primarily to people of African, Native American, Asian, Latino/a, or Middle Eastern descent. Many push back on the term *people of color* by rightly pointing out that White people have "color" too—which, of course, they do! White people are not the color of snow, just as Black people aren't the color of the midnight sky. At the same time, the term *people of color* has resonated with many because it helps these groups enjoy solidarity with one another. It's also noteworthy that the term has precedent. For example, Martin Luther King, Jr., used the phrase *citizens of color* in his 1963 "I Have a Dream" speech. So, for now, we'll go with it.

A final note: As of this writing, there is no general agreement on whether the words *Black* and *White* (or the related terms of color) should be capitalized. Many have given compelling reasons for why one, both, or neither word should be capitalized. For simplicity and consistency, this text will capitalize both terms.

LET THE JOURNEY BEGIN!

So, let's wrap this up. Why should Christians of this generation bother to deepen our understanding of ongoing racial realities and inequities? We do so because we are disciples of Jesus Christ. We do so to experience more of Jesus. And we do so to further Christ's mission in the world.

Remember, too, that while *racism* is a stain on God's creation, *ethnicity* is a God-ordained cultural identity that God delights in to bring glory to himself and riches to everyone in his kingdom—

including you. Those who take steps to dismantle racism will undoubtedly discover new opportunities to enjoy more of the surprising riches of God's colorful kingdom.

As you go deeper now into this journey of color-courageous discipleship, I pray that you will be surprised by how God works—both to bring greater shalom to your corner of the world and to draw you closer to Jesus Christ!

THINK ABOUT IT

1. As we begin this journey, what are some of your own thoughts about what race and racism have to do with discipleship?

2. What do you understand so far about the difference between being "nonracist" and being "antiracist"? Why does it matter?

3. In your own words, what is the difference between race and ethnicity? Why is that distinction helpful? What are some riches of ethnic diversity that you have experienced or would like to experience?

4. What hopes and concerns do you have for the color-courageous discipleship journey?

5. How do you imagine that you might experience Jesus more deeply on this journey?

A CHRIST-CENTERED APPROACH TO ANTIRACISM

> For God was pleased to have all his fullness dwell
> in [Christ], and through him to reconcile to himself
> all things ... by making peace through his blood,
> shed on the cross.
>
> **COLOSSIANS 1:19–20**

As I make my way through the corridors of my office, I am keenly aware of my beating heart. It's time for my very first performance review with my boss at my new job. Butterflies break-dance in my stomach as I wonder: *I've given this my all, and I've done okay . . . but what have I missed?*

Quick rewind: Earlier in the year, I jumped from leading discipleship at a thriving local church to leading discipleship for an entire denomination of churches across North America. And to be honest, it was a steep jump—I started as *both* the youngest executive and the first person of color to lead discipleship for our movement. So, you better believe that I was giving the job my all. My main motivation, of course, was to glorify God. But if I'm honest, I was also striving to prove that those who took the chance to hire me—young, Black, female me—had made the right choice.

Here I am. *Inhale.* I knock, and my boss ushers me in with his usual warm welcome. We take our seats—the senior White male on one side, the junior Black female on the other. I'm eager, as usual, to be accepted. We engage in small talk. "How is your family?" he inquires. "Have you found a church you like?" It's clear that he cares—about me, my family, and my flourishing.

The evaluation begins. I am calm. I am on top of my game. He showers me with affirmations. Yet my heart is clenched. *Okay . . . but what have I missed? What else is coming?* I finally sense him shifting gears to constructive feedback mode, and I brace myself. *Have I not been relational enough as a manager? Have I done enough for our churches? Do people appreciate my work?*

Finally, he begins: "Michelle, I have noticed a pattern. . . . It seems that most White people within our movement appreciate you . . . yet there are some Black folks who are not fans. Why do you think that is?"

What happens next is a blur. My confident facade shatters, and to my horror, I erupt in tears. Now hear me: I don't cry at work. Nevertheless, today my tears flow, and flow, and continue to flow as we press through the conversation. I struggle to remain in the present as I am pulled back to the past. Once again, I see my childhood bullies, parading by in quick succession. They taunt me again in this moment with the accusation that I am an "Oreo cookie"—Black on the outside, White on the inside, and (I fear) ultimately unacceptable to all sides. Once again, I am a little girl, frightened and ashamed. Will it never stop? *Never enough, never enough. I have no home. I am haunted by race. I'm not White, so obviously I can't be "White enough" for Whites. And, apparently, I can't be "Black enough" for Blacks either. So . . . who am I? How do I navigate this race thing? What am I supposed to do?*

When it comes to race, many of us, like me, have questions. Questions like: *Who is God calling me to be? What am I supposed to do in this moment . . . and where do I even begin?* For disciples of

Jesus, the answer is as simple as it is deep. *As disciples of Jesus, we start with Jesus.*

In my own life, I brought my racial challenges to Jesus . . . *eventually.* Honestly, when I was growing up, I was never really discipled to talk to Jesus about race. My Christian discipleship had been characterized by a color-blind approach rather than one that could be called color-courageous. So this was a journey that I needed to take without a map—which hopefully you won't have to do!

Back to my story: I left work for the day soon after my dam of tears had burst. On the drive home, I wailed inside my car, soaking my steering wheel with tears. It took a long, long time for me to move past my pain and discomfort so that I could be open to further learning and growth.

Yet God was patient with me. (He's like that, you know.) He whispered: "Hey there, discipleship leader. Remember that at the end of the day, *race is a matter of discipleship too.*" God also reminded me that the journey of color-courageous discipleship, like any other, starts and ends *with Jesus.*

If you identify as a disciple of Jesus Christ, I invite you to restart your racial discipleship journey with Jesus now. When it comes to race, ask your king: *What am I missing? What do I need to learn? How can I grow?* Jesus loves you, and he will show you! I guarantee that Jesus is excited to disciple you in new ways.

CHRIST-CENTERED ANTIRACISM:
JESUS AS LORD AND SAVIOR

When I was still in my twenties, I had a really special ministry opportunity. I got to volunteer at Billy Graham's 417th and final evangelistic outreach. It was a historic moment. That summer of 2005, over 240,000 people descended upon Flushing Meadows Corona Park in New York City to hear the legendary preacher proclaim the gospel for the final time. You could feel the excitement in the air.

BILLY GRAHAM

Billy Graham (1918–2018) was one of the most famous evangelists who ever lived. In fact, Graham preached to more people in person than anyone else in the history of Christianity! He did so by launching and preaching at hundreds of evangelistic rallies and "crusades" (multiple-day outreach events) over the course of his life. Graham was also a spiritual adviser to U.S. presidents. In fact, he provided spiritual counsel to every president from Harry S. Truman to Barack Obama. Perhaps you have heard that Graham was a great preacher, but did you know that he was also a civil rights advocate? He rejected racial segregation at a time when segregation was the norm. What's more, he insisted that his crusades be racially integrated starting from 1953. In 1957, Graham invited Martin Luther King, Jr., to preach jointly with him at a revival in New York City. Due to Graham's unwavering commitment to the gospel over the course of a lifetime, more than three million people have responded to the invitation to accept Jesus Christ as Savior and Lord.

Like many others, I had been trained by Cru, an interdenominational Christian organization, and the Billy Graham Evangelistic Association to share the gospel using the well-known phrase *Would you like to accept Jesus as Lord and Savior?* Perhaps you or someone you know first accepted Jesus by saying yes to this question.

You know, "Jesus is Lord and Savior" is actually a great summary of the **gospel**. The word *gospel* means "good news," and our good news is that Jesus Christ is Lord and Savior. Of course, the phrase *Lord and Savior* did not originate with Billy Graham. It comes to us directly from the Scriptures (for example, 2 Peter 3:18). The good news that Jesus is Lord and Savior never gets old or irrelevant. Of course, there is a pivotal point at which many disciples say yes to Jesus as Lord and Savior for the first time. But the reality is that our journey will continue to bring life to the extent that we continue to say yes every day and in every way. Disciples are called to both start *and sustain* every new discipleship adventure—including the adventure of color-courageous discipleship—with the good news that Jesus is Lord and Savior.

INVITATION #1: WHAT DOES IT MEAN FOR COLOR-COURAGEOUS DISCIPLES TO HONOR JESUS AS LORD?

Is it possible to produce a list of the most influential people of all time? That's debatable, but many have risen to the challenge. Steven Skiena, a professor of computer science at Stony Brook University, did just that.[1] In the same way that Google identifies and ranks web pages, Skiena gathered all the data and used formulas to rank more than one thousand of the most historically significant people in all areas of human endeavor.

You may not be surprised to see that Jesus came out number one. But see, that's the problem! We have gotten so used to Jesus that we are no longer baffled by him. How in the world did this poor man who was basically born as a nobody come to dominate world history?

Six of the ten figures on this list commanded armies. Jesus was born in a sty, preached peace, and then was executed as a criminal—at which point most of his followers promptly deserted him. The remaining three figures revolutionized the world primarily through the power of their pens. Jesus wrote nothing.

MOST HISTORICALLY SIGNIFICANT PEOPLE

1. Jesus
2. Napoleon
3. Muhammad
4. William Shakespeare
5. Abraham Lincoln
6. George Washington
7. Adolf Hitler
8. Aristotle
9. Alexander the Great
10. Thomas Jefferson

More than two billion people, or roughly one-third of the world's population, identify as his followers. The Bible, the book that tells his story, is by far the bestselling book of all time. Time itself orbits around the birth of Christ. When we say that it's the year 2030, for example, we are acknowledging that it's been about 2,030 years since Jesus was here with us in person.

You might imagine that the famous general Napoleon, notorious for his gargantuan ego, would be miffed about ranking second. On the contrary: Napoleon, too, marveled at how Jesus outshone him. At the end of his life, Napoleon seemed obsessed with the question of how the lowly carpenter from Nazareth continued to dazzle after death. He confessed with wonder: "Alexander, Caesar, Charlemagne, and myself, founded empires. But upon what did we rest the creations of our genius? Upon *force.* Jesus Christ alone founded His empire upon *love;* and at this hour millions of men would die for Him. . . . What a proof of the divinity of Christ!"[2]

The only reasonable explanation for Jesus's powerful and persistent impact is that he truly was who he said he was: the Son of God and Lord of all.

NAPOLEON

Napoleon Bonaparte (1769–1821) was a French military leader who gained timeless fame by conquering much of Europe in the early nineteenth century. He is known for having a big ego—he even eventually crowned himself as an emperor! But of course, like everyone else, Napoleon was only human. After suffering a final battle at Waterloo, he was exiled to the island of Saint Helena, where he died at the age of fifty-one. While there, he apparently had plenty of time to compare himself to others—including Jesus. He was especially impressed by how Jesus was able to inspire such allegiance and transform the world ... *without waging a single battle.*

Napoleon Crossing the Alps, Jacques Louis David, 1800

Fun Fact: When we joke that someone has a "Napoleon complex," it means that they are a very short, domineering person. But actually, Napoleon wasn't *that* short—he was roughly five feet six inches, about the average height at that time. He may have gotten a reputation for being a little guy because of the way he was portrayed in a number of cartoons at the time. Bummer!

The book of Colossians presents an even more astonishing vision of Jesus. The apostle Paul was concerned that the Colossians' understanding of the supremacy of Jesus Christ had been compromised. Paul wanted them to understand that Jesus was *greater*—greater than anything or anyone else they could ever devote their lives to. That's why Paul wrote this letter—to persuade the Colossian disciples to recommit to Jesus as Lord.

Of course, bullying doesn't really motivate anybody over the long term ("Worship Jesus or else!"). So Paul didn't take that approach. What he understood is that the human soul *is* deeply motivated by beauty. We will exalt Jesus as Lord in an all-encompassing way to the extent that we become enraptured by his all-encompassing beauty. Paul understood this. This is why the beating heart of his letter to the Colossians was not a speech but a song. In fact, many believe that Colossians 1:15–20 is actually taken from an ancient Christian song that gloried in the supremacy of Christ. It says this:

> The Son is the image of the invisible God, the firstborn over all creation. For in him all things were created: things in heaven and on earth, visible and invisible, whether thrones or powers or rulers or authorities; all things have been created through him and for him. He is before all things, and in him all things hold together. . . . He is the beginning and the firstborn from among the dead, *so that in everything he might have the supremacy.* (Colossians 1:15–18)

The Colossian Christ-hymn woos our hearts with a fresh revelation of Jesus as Lord. It celebrates Jesus as God-with-us, the exquisite image of the invisible God. Humans suffer from an unquenchable heart-longing that nothing in this world can satisfy. Perhaps you, too, have experienced this heart-longing. Earthly beauty can provide temporary relief to our longing, of course—birds exchanging love songs in the brightness of dawn, endless ocean waves reaching beyond the horizon, fireflies suspended across boundless fields. And yet our nagging longing lingers still. The truth is that our yearning for beauty will only be satisfied in glory when we see the face of God—God, who is the source and creator of all beauty, the beauty to which all other beauties point. But—marvel of marvels!—we can enjoy a glimpse of our gorgeous God now in the face of Jesus Christ.

As disciples, we frequently say yes to Jesus in some areas of our lives while holding back in others. We are afraid to trust Jesus with the *whole* of our lives. But just as Jesus urged his twelve disciples, so he continues to urge us now: "Take courage! It is I. Don't be afraid" (Matthew 14:27). The Colossians hymn reveals that Jesus Christ is Lord not only because he is the image of the invisible God but also because he is, wondrously, the creator of the cosmos. In him, all things hold together and find their meaning—including race and ethnicity. Because Jesus is Lord of all, we have every reason to take courage. We have every reason to honor Christ as the leader of every part of our lives, including race.

When it comes to matters of race, Jesus invites us again to courageously say yes to him alone as Lord. Jesus is, truly, the only one who deserves it!

Invitation #2: What Does It Mean for Color-Courageous Disciples to Honor Jesus as Savior?

After celebrating Jesus as Lord, the Colossian hymn exalts him as Savior—the one who rescues us from sin and death by his shed blood and reconciles us to God.

> For God was pleased to have all his fullness dwell in him, and through him to reconcile to himself all things, whether things on earth or things in heaven, by making peace through his blood, shed on the cross. (Colossians 1:19–20)

The name *Jesus* means "the Lord saves." But what, exactly, does Jesus save us from? An angel instructed Mary to name her son Jesus because "he will save his people *from their sins*" (Matthew 1:21). That's what Jesus achieved for us through his death on the cross. If we hope to experience the shalom that God intended in the world and in our own lives, we've got to figure out how to deal with the problem of sin.

What is sin? **Sin** happens whenever we choose our will instead of God's will. We sin whenever we take actions that are contrary to God's design. By the way, the Bible says that we are all guilty of sin to varying degrees (Romans 3:23). Unfortunately, the consequence of living in ways that are contrary to God's design is brokenness, destruction, and death—for us and all creation (Genesis 3; Romans 6:23). That's why we desperately need a Savior! *Jesus is that Savior.* As the Son of God, he came and lived a perfect life without sin. At the end of his life, he died for us, shedding his own blood to save us from our sins—all because God loves us! (John 3:16).

> He was pierced for our rebellion, crushed for our sins. He was beaten so we could be whole. He was whipped so we could be healed. (Isaiah 53:5, NLT)

By the way, I absolutely love that the Hebrew word for "whole" in this verse is *shalom*. When Jesus saves from sin, the outcome is a restoration of shalom.

If we're honest, though, it's actually hard to admit that we need a savior. This, too, requires courage—the courage of humility. Needing a savior implies that we are, well, needy. It implies that we are sinful. Broken. Helpless without God. *All of these things are true.* Jesus freed us from the *power* of sin, yes. But we will still struggle with the *presence* of sin until Jesus returns. To make meaningful progress on the racial discipleship journey, we as disciples must deeply understand the brokenness in our own lives and in every dimension of creation.

Speaking of which, did you know that sin is not just an *indi-*

vidual problem? Human sin has led not only to a broken relationship with God but to brokenness on every level of creation. In a similar way, when it comes to the sin of racism, the problem is not just that individual people have bad attitudes. The problem is that all creation is broken on every level and needs to be reconciled (healed or fixed) on every level. I resonate with how George Yancey puts it in his book *Beyond Racial Gridlock:* "The problem of racism is the problem of sin."[3] Everything has been broken by sin, and only God can put everything back together again. That is what **reconciliation** in our Colossian Christ-song is all about: *making all that is broken whole again.* In fact, the song concludes with a reconciliation celebration, showing us how God is making things right again on every level of creation through Jesus Christ.

What do I mean by "every level" of creation? Let's draw this out. We can envision the levels of creation as four concentric circles: *individual, interpersonal, systemic,* and *cosmic*—each with deep implications for how racism works and how to uproot it.[4] Too often, we have sought to deal with racism on only one or two of these levels when we really need to engage *every* level. All four dimensions of creation are broken, and ultimately, all four can be fully and finally reconciled only through the blood of Jesus Christ.

Now, a little exercise. In the first chapters of Genesis, we can progressively trace how sin broke God's good world on every level—chapter by chapter. Let's take a look.

Individual level (read Genesis 3:1–10). I first became a follower of Jesus as a little girl. I knelt before a high window and lifted my head to the sky in prayer. As a shaft of light cascaded down on me, I asked Jesus to forgive my sins. Of course, what I had in mind as a child was personal sin. Yet I suspect that many disciples, regardless of age, continue to consider sin primarily on a personal level. And that makes sense because that's also where Scripture begins with sin—on the *individual level.*

Four Levels of Creation

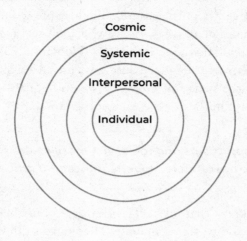

Our story—the story of everything—began with beauty, abundance, and delight (Genesis 1–2). Tragically, though, the trouble begins as early as Genesis chapter 3. That's when the first humans rejected God in the hopes of becoming "like God" themselves (3:5). Our ancestors' decision to distrust and disobey God put them squarely at odds with the Creator, and we continue to live with the consequences. On an individual level, Adam and Eve sense an immediate change and rush to cover their sin with fig leaves. This is a sad and pitiful picture of the never-ending human attempt to hide the guilt and shame that alienate us from God and one another. As individuals, we are now broken on every human level. We suffer from emotional distress, mental illness, and physical ailments. Worst of all, our connection with God has been broken. God created us to enjoy endless life. But instead, we now awaken each morning trapped on a high-speed train barreling inevitably toward our final destination—the grave.

What does individual brokenness have to do with our racial

discipleship journey? The answer is that we cannot make meaningful progress when it comes to race until we courageously comprehend the depths of our individual brokenness. This is true for disciples of all races. As we will soon see, racial oppressors and racial victims alike are sinners (Romans 3:23); we are all called to repentance and grace. Just as we are all equally dignified in reflecting the image of God, we are also equally in need of forgiveness and healing at the foot of the cross.

Racial oppressors and racial victims alike are sinners; we are all called to repentance and grace.

Did you know that sin has even impacted our ability to think and perceive the world accurately? Theologians call this the **noetic effect of sin.** *Noetic* comes from the Greek word for "intellect." This is one explanation for our human inclination toward unconscious bias and racism, even from a very early age. Even if we don't *mean* to treat people differently based on race, we often do so unconsciously anyway! But we shouldn't be surprised. This is just one more way that sin has broken our ability to love others well and treat people equally.

Interpersonal level (read Genesis 3:11–4:16). As I grew up, I came to comprehend sin in a more relational way. When I experienced racial bullying for the first time, for example, I came to understand just how badly *hurt people hurt people.* But even more importantly, God gradually opened my eyes to the ways in which my *own* sins were spoiling many of the relationships that mattered most to me.

In a similar way, the Genesis story traces the cancerous spread of sin from the *individual level* to the *interpersonal level.* Conflict erupts between Adam and Eve, and soon we observe how sin spreads to their children and their children's children. We watch with dismay as sin spoils interpersonal relationships through jealousy, abuse, and even violence. Now marriage ends in divorce. Friendships become mired in misunderstanding. Family feuds fester in unforgiveness.

When it comes to racism, Christians have probably paid the *most* attention so far to how racism impacts our interpersonal relationships. Interpersonal racism and prejudice are easy to see, and most people no longer tolerate this kind of behavior. For example, most Christians no longer approve of racial jokes and slurs, join White supremacist groups like the Ku Klux Klan, or believe that people of color are not as good as White people. Obviously, that's progress!

However, it's still critical for us to understand that interpersonal racial brokenness takes other forms as well—and those are the forms that are far more pervasive today. Interpersonal racism is *not* always loud and obvious. It can be subtle as well.

Systemic level (read Genesis 4:17–26). When I was a child, I remember asking my mother why all my (mostly White) friends hosted birthday parties at their homes—but we never did. She told me that she feared my friends would not want to visit our part of town. So many questions followed: *What was wrong with our part of town? And, by extension, what was wrong with us? Why did we all live in different parts of town anyway?* I didn't have the words at the time, but clearly, I was beginning to witness the effects of larger systemic dynamics at work. Of course, we all understand systemic brokenness at *some* level. Again, whenever we watch the news, we are reminded that it's not only humans—but also *systems created by humans*—that are defective. It is only recently that God has helped me understand the *depths* of the systemic brokenness of our world, as well as how I have unwittingly perpetuated that brokenness.

Systemic brokenness is an ancient affliction. We see it develop as we watch sin's infection spread to Cain's descendants and, through them, to the city they founded. After Cain kills Abel, he wanders east, further away from his parents and "from the LORD's presence" (4:16). He establishes a family in the land of Nod and builds a city there. I have lived and worked in cities around the world, from New York City to Minneapolis to Quito to Hong Kong, and I can testify: Every human city is simultaneously glorious and galling. Cain's prosperous first city was no different. Yet, even as the constructive creativity of the city grew, so too did its destructive creativity. As the city grew and multiplied, so too did oppression and violence (4:19–24).

God is calling disciples to awaken to the ways in which sin has subtly yet deeply impacted not just our individual relationships but also our communities—our organizations, institutions, cities, and even nations. Our cities are flawed because we are flawed. Our organizations are racially broken because we are racially broken. Systemic racism is, quite simply, what racial brokenness and sin look like in the systems that people have created together—systems like business, education, government, and more. But it operates differently: The power of systemic racism is that it stubbornly persists as a problem for racial minorities while remaining invisible to the racial majority.

Here's the thing: *The antiracist awakening of our generation is mostly about our awakening to systemic racism.* I am excited to look more closely with you at systemic racism in the next chapter.

The antiracist awakening of our generation is mostly about our awakening to systemic racism.

Cosmic level (read Genesis 5–7). Ultimately sin has a cosmic impact—it infects everyone, spreads everywhere, and taints everything. Nature itself has become a constant source of frustration and pain (3:18; 5:28–29).

Many generations after the Fall, Lamech named his son *Noah,* which means "comfort." Lamech hoped that somehow Noah would "comfort us in the labor and painful toil of our hands caused by the ground the LORD has cursed" (5:29). Unfortunately, as humankind increased in numbers across the earth, they only increased in wickedness. And when God looked down at all the evil and suffering, God "was very sad that he had made human beings on the earth. His heart was filled with pain" (Genesis 6:6, NIRV). We tend to think that God brought the flood upon the earth because he was *mad,* but here the Bible tells us he did this because he was *sad.* It was deep sorrow that compelled our Creator to cleanse the earth with a flood. Our sin has cosmic dimensions, and eventually, the whole world must be cleansed and reconciled.

As color-courageous disciples, we will be effective to the extent that we understand that racial brokenness has cosmic dimensions. There is a real cosmic battle raging behind human events. The Scriptures reveal that there are larger **powers and principalities** at war against God and that as disciples we are called to combat these enemies in God's power (Ephesians 6:12, NKJV). *Powers and principalities* refer to real, intentional evil that is at work in the world to destroy God's good purposes. What's more, evil powers and principalities refer not only to demonic forces but also to deceptive and destructive *ideas* like racism.

Committing to color-courageous discipleship means working to identify and dismantle racial lies wherever we encounter them. Too often, we find ourselves raging against one another. But in reality "our struggle is *not* against flesh and blood" (Ephesians 6:12). Thankfully, we have cause to rejoice because Christ is supreme over all powers (Colossians 1:15–18). In the end, Jesus wins. But in the meantime, color-courageous disciples are invited to partner with Christ in his work of cosmic reconciliation.

To summarize: Saying yes again to Jesus as Savior when it comes to race means acknowledging that our world is racially broken on every level and that we need Jesus to save and reconcile us on every level—starting with ourselves. Honestly, it takes real courage to admit that we cannot save the world! To become

START WITH THE *REAL* JESUS

As we start with Jesus, let's also remember the importance of starting with the *real* Jesus. Our view of the real Jesus has been obscured over many years. Every generation and culture tends to reimagine Jesus in their own image. Let's take a moment to recall just a few key facts about who Jesus actually was:

- a person of color (not of European descent, but a Middle Eastern Jew)
- a member of a marginalized and oppressed minority group (under the Roman Empire)
- a refugee (whose parents desperately fled to Egypt to save his life)
- a blue-collar worker (trained as a carpenter—not an elite religious scholar)
- a convicted criminal on death row (tried and sentenced according to the law)

We have gotten so used to our contemporary conceptions of Jesus that sometimes the real Jesus eludes us. Jesus is a surprising figure in every way, and so it goes without saying—our color-courageous discipleship journey will also yield some surprises!

effective agents of racial shalom, we must learn to humbly say yes again and again to Jesus as Savior.

COLOR-COURAGEOUS DISCIPLES: RECONCILED TO RECONCILE

We've been exploring why it is vital to start our racial discipleship journey with Jesus as Lord and Savior. In short, we do so because "Christ is all, and is in all" (Colossians 3:11). Jesus invites us to say yes again to him as *Lord,* making sure to honor him as supreme in every area of our lives, including race and ethnicity. He also invites us to say yes again to him as *Savior,* which means humbly admitting our racial brokenness and neediness on every level. In all things, including our color-courageous ministry efforts, Jesus Christ must remain central and supreme for disciples.

Let's remember: According to the ancient understanding, being a disciple meant following a *particular person.* That's why I believe that only as we recommit to the person of Jesus can our pursuit of antiracism become a *discipleship* journey. I want to encourage you: As you pursue antiracism for Jesus, remember that you are not working for some*thing* (antiracism) but for some*one* (Jesus). If you do this, antiracism will become a courageous expression of following Jesus himself, our cherished Lord and Savior.

> **Disciples are called not only to serve Jesus but also to allow Jesus to serve through us.**

What's more, disciples are called not only to *serve Jesus* but also to *allow Jesus to serve through us.* God has invited us to become "Christ's ambassadors" in his all-encompassing "ministry of reconciliation":

> All this is from God, who reconciled us to himself through Christ and gave us the ministry of reconciliation: that God was reconciling the world to himself in Christ, not counting people's sins against them. And he has committed to us the message of reconciliation. We are therefore Christ's ambassadors, *as though God were making his appeal through us.* We implore you on Christ's behalf: Be reconciled to God. (2 Corinthians 5:18–20)

This is a breathtaking privilege. As disciples, God has promised to work in us and through us to bring reconciliation to the world. Through the power of the Holy Spirit, we are now *reconciled reconcilers*—not just on one level, but on every level of creation. God invites us to reconnect *individuals* to himself through his provision of forgiveness and healing. He invites us to restore *interpersonal* relationships as grace-givers and peacemakers. He invites us to dismantle *systemic* racism in communities and organizations. And he invites us to combat *cosmic* evil forces as we identify false ideologies and join with all the saints in prayer against the evil powers and principalities of our world. As disciples, we are **ambassadors of reconciliation.** We are reconciled to reconcile! This is the power of Christ at work through us.

Although I didn't realize it at first, that fateful afternoon in my boss's office turned out to be an important step on my own journey of racial discipleship. After I emerged from the fog of my initial pain and discomfort, I saw the truth: *I have room to grow.* Yes, I am a Black woman, and I have experienced racism. Yet I was also reared in predominantly White, well-resourced contexts, which means that there were many important aspects of systemic injustice that I have not experienced. That day, I truly began to understand that I can do more to help.

I clearly recognized the voice of Christ calling me to engage more deeply in color-courageous discipleship for the sake of the church and the world. Now, I have to be honest: It was both a terrifying and mystifying invitation! I wasn't even sure what it would entail. What I did know, though, was that it would be a precious opportunity to face my fears and grow. So, despite my questions and qualms, I said yes to a new discipleship journey with Jesus, holding tightly to him as Savior and Lord.

As he invited me then, so he continues to invite us now:

I am the Alpha and the Omega,
the First and the Last,
the Beginning and the End.
Yes! That is why you can take courage.
It is I. Do not be afraid.
Instead of wasting time with fear, be sure of this:
I am with you always, even to the end of the age.[5]

THINK ABOUT IT

1. According to the study in this chapter, Jesus is the most influential person in history! Does that surprise you? Why or why not? Where and how have you seen Jesus's impact on the world?

2. When you admit that you still need Jesus as Savior, it means that you understand that you still need his help. Where do you need more help from Jesus today?

3. Christians say that Jesus is Lord, but we don't always live that way. Why do you think it's so much easier to let Jesus lead some parts of our lives but not other parts?

4. Where have you seen the brokenness of the world at the individual, interpersonal, systemic, and cosmic levels? Which level(s) would you like to learn more about and why?

5. What questions do you have about the disciples' call to be "ambassadors of reconciliation"? What do you find most interesting or exciting about this call?

COLOR-COURAGEOUS
PARADIGM SHIFTS

Over the years, I have been captivated by this rallying cry: let's make disciples *who make* disciples! We don't want to be disciples who shrink or stagnate—we want to multiply!

Yet someone once asked some questions that gave me pause: "Okay, yes, but what kind of disciples are we making? What if we're making disciples who are jerks? I mean, if we're making disciples but those disciples aren't actually much like Christ, what's the point?"

Wow. Very true. Yes, healthy things grow and multiply. But so do unhealthy things—like cancer! The church needs growth, but more specifically, the church needs *healthy* growth: Christlike disciples who make Christlike disciples. Color-courageous disciples who make color-courageous disciples.

Here's a striking illustration for you. Did you know that one of the earliest slave ships was named *Jesus*? Listen to this:

Two of the first English ships to carry West Africans to the New World had ominous names: *Jesus* and *Minion*. . . . Both ships served the same purpose. . . . Forced aboard *Jesus,* African men and women probably had no idea that the ship bore the name of a man who had been crucified fifteen centuries earlier. They probably had no idea that the vessel outfitted with guns, chains, and dungeons was named for the "prince of peace" who had come to "set the captives free."[1]

Needless to say, a label does not necessarily equate to reality! Just as a ship with the label *Jesus* does not necessarily reflect who Jesus is, so a person with the label *Jesus-follower* does not necessarily do what Jesus does. That is why, to reflect Christ more deeply, deeper discipleship is needed.

What do I mean by "deeper" discipleship? Let's reimagine discipleship as a diamond. There is a way in which all diamonds are the same—for example, all diamonds are crystallized forms of carbon. Yet we also know that some diamonds are far more brilliant than others. In fact, the word *brilliance* is a technical term that gemologists use to measure a diamond's shine. All diamonds sparkle. But the more facets (cut surfaces) a diamond has, the more brilliantly it will shine. The "round brilliant" cut is the most brilliant diamond cut of all; its fifty-eight facets beautifully refract white light in multiple directions, thus achieving its unparalleled dazzling effect.

In the same way, healthy discipleship is composed of multiple discipleship facets, which we can also refer to as *discipleship dimensions* or *paradigms.* All who follow Jesus are being shaped into his image to some degree. Yet some will more brilliantly reflect his image than others—because they reflect *more dimensions* of who Jesus has called us to be. This is what mature color-courageous disciples are like: diamonds of a round brilliant cut, beautifully reflecting more facets of who Jesus calls us to be.

---

*Color-courageous disciples will reflect **more** dimensions of who Jesus calls us to be.*

In part 2, we will consider four different discipleship paradigms that Jesus calls us to embrace in order to reflect him more brilliantly. To be clear, these are not *new* discipleship paradigms, but they are discipleship paradigms that have been *underemphasized* in recent times in the Western church. Unfortunately, our underemphasis of these general discipleship paradigms has made it easier for racial inequity, in particular, to persist. That is one reason why racial inequity has persisted in the church, and it also explains why our discipleship has been less than color-courageous. The truth is that we have some major recovery work to do when it comes to reflecting all that Jesus calls us to be. *Same discipleship, but fresh dimensions.*

The church does not only need disciples who make disciples. The church also needs Christlike disciples who make Christlike disciples; ambassadors of reconciliation who make ambassadors of reconciliation; and color-courageous disciples who make color-courageous disciples.

Friend, let's seek to shine with the full brilliance of Jesus Christ. For *this* is how God's kingdom comes.

DISCIPLESHIP AS AWAKENING

Open Your Eyes to the Myth of Equality

> One of the great liabilities of history is that all too many
> people fail to remain awake.
>
> —MARTIN LUTHER KING, JR., *WHERE DO WE GO FROM HERE?*

It's the middle of the night, and the disciples are with Jesus in the Garden of Gethsemane. It's an important night, but unfortunately the disciples don't know that. They don't know that this is the night before Jesus's crucifixion. For the Twelve, it's just another night with Jesus. The thing is, it's also a *really late* night and the disciples' eyes are getting heavy. Jesus has asked them to stay up and pray. They do for a little while, but they also don't understand why staying up to pray on this *particular* night is such a big deal. Jesus is always saying things that don't make much sense to the disciples. So, when Jesus isn't looking, they begin to doze off. Suddenly, catastrophe! Soldiers burst onto the scene, coming to arrest Jesus!

In the Garden of Gethsemane, the disciples failed to do the one thing that Jesus needed most. They learned the hard way that discipleship isn't *just* about believing what Jesus said and doing his work. Jesus urged his disciples three times to stay awake

The Agony in the Garden, right panel of the predella of
the San Zeno Altarpiece, 1455, National Gallery, London

and join him to prepare for what was coming. But each time, the disciples drifted off to sleep. As a result, they were utterly unprepared when the soldiers came for Jesus. And then, when Jesus was arrested, the disciples even deserted him—something I'm sure they never dreamed they would do.

All this goes to show that, sadly, the disciples snoozed right through one of their greatest opportunities to partner with Jesus. That night, the disciples learned firsthand what it means to faithfully follow Jesus: to *stay awake*.

> **That night, the disciples learned firsthand what it means to faithfully follow Jesus: to stay awake.**

Time and again, the Scriptures call for awakening. And guess what? It is usually believers—*not* unbelievers—who are urged to wake up! Apparently, you can be a fully committed follower of Jesus and yet still remain fast asleep in important ways. This is what the Bible says about it:

For you were once darkness, but now you are light in the Lord. Live as children of light . . . and find out what pleases the Lord. Have nothing to do with the fruitless deeds of darkness, but rather expose them. . . . This is why it is said: "Wake up, sleeper, rise from the dead, and Christ will shine on you." (Ephesians 5:8, 10–11, 14)

It goes without saying that sleep is *not* a bad thing in itself. God designed us to sleep, and God grants sleep to those he loves (Psalm 127:2). Nevertheless, we all know that there are times when falling asleep will get you into trouble, like when you're driving down a dark and curvy highway at two o'clock in the morning, for example!

By definition, when we are asleep, we cannot remain attentive to what is unfolding around us in the real world. We are immersed in a comfortable darkness. We inhabit a dream world that seems true but is not. Now, being unconscious is fine . . . unless there is something dangerous happening around you! And according to the Scriptures, there *is* something dangerous—something spiritually evil—unfolding in the darkness around us. This is why disciples are encouraged to stay awake, expose the "deeds of darkness," and live courageously as children of light (Ephesians 5:7–16).

Evil and darkness are actually all around us. It helps to recognize the true *nature* of evil. Evil often seems harmless. Normal. Acceptable. At times evil is like an enchanting lullaby, singing us to sleep. To wake up, we must become fully aware of the evil around us and listen for how Jesus wants us to resist it. Discipleship is, at heart, a journey of awakening.

AWAKENING TO THE MYTH OF EQUALITY

Not many people can say that their high school graduation made front-page news. But mine did. When I graduated as the first

African American valedictorian of my predominantly White school district, it earned me a headline on the front page of the local newspaper!

Me . . . graduating as first Black
valedictorian
PHOTO BY ISLAND PHOTOGRAPHY

Growing up, I was educated in a well-resourced school district on Long Island, and it set me up for success. But it's only now that I realize how fortunate I was. My parents grew up across the street from one another in the Bronx, a part of New York City. They were both descendants of slavery by way of the South (my dad) and the Caribbean (my mom). After they married, my parents purchased a home on Long Island through a homeownership program for lower-income families. The greatest reward from that move was the opportunity for my brothers and me to access a wealthier school district, something we would not have had in the South Bronx.

Still, don't get me wrong: My childhood had its challenges. We lived in a working-class, Black part of town surrounded by richer White neighborhoods. So, I grew up with a slew of White friends whom I loved, but I also inwardly resented many of them for their fancier homes, cars, clothes, summer camps, and vacations. For years I felt "homeless"—neither fitting in racially with Whites nor culturally with Blacks. I have already mentioned how, when I excelled at school, Black bullies accused me of being an Oreo. Day after day, I woke up in the darkness of the early morning and thought that even death would be better than going back to school to face them. It was agonizing. For so long, people who looked like me had struggled for opportunities to succeed. Why, then, were some in the community traumatizing those among us who *were* finally making it?

While some might have responded to such harassment by ditching their studies to fit in, I buried myself in books. "By reading and studying hard," my mentors promised, "you will leave the haters behind and achieve the life that you have always dreamed of." So, study hard I did.

When I was a kid, my idol was Clair Huxtable. She was a Black, sassy TV character on *The Cosby Show.* She had a law career, five kids, great hair, *and* a snazzy townhouse in Brooklyn. I thought that if I studied hard enough, I could be her. I knew I could be her! Over time, the bullies left me alone, and I excelled. In the end, I achieved the feat of finishing first in my class and winning thousands of dollars in scholarships. Later, after graduating from New York University, I went to work at a prestigious bank called Goldman Sachs. The formula had worked for me. I was well on my way: Study hard, receive rewards, and live like Clair Huxtable!

Only after college did I begin to realize that this "foolproof" formula for success in life might not actually work for everyone. This is when my own antiracist racial awakening truly began.

While working at Goldman, I volunteered to teach economics for a day at an under-resourced, inner-city school. As I rode the subway uptown, I was excited for the opportunity to inspire students whom I had imagined to be mini versions of me.

The school that I visited was mostly Black and Brown, and I was shocked by the conditions I witnessed there. I honestly never imagined that a school like this one could exist in the United States of America: dilapidated facilities, dark corridors, over-crowded classrooms with desks spilling over into the hallways, rowdy and troubled kids who made it impossible for others to learn, even if they wanted to. It was as if I had crossed over an invisible border into a developing nation. I'll tell you this much: This school certainly did *not* feel like one located in the most prosperous country the world has ever known. I stumbled through the lesson I had prepared, but honestly, it wasn't much use.

If a society's systems persistently result in
different outcomes for different races,
you have a racialized society.

My understanding of the world to that point had been de-fined by my version of the American dream formula that I previously described: Study hard, receive rewards, and live like Clair Huxtable. It only took one day of teaching at this school to ex-plode that formula. The formula itself is not necessarily *wrong,* but it simply *does not apply in the same way* to everyone. Questions swirled: *When I was growing up, what if the conditions of my school didn't make me want to learn . . . but escape? What if my education had been—inherently—unequal?*

Although that experience happened to me many years ago now, I have never recovered. Nor should I. A recent story in *The New York Times* once again left me speechless. It was entitled "25-Year-Old Textbooks and Holes in the Ceiling: Inside America's Public Schools."[1] With renewed horror, I realized that the tattered biology textbook featured was the same textbook that I had used in my own biology class roughly twenty-five years ago.

My journey toward color-courageous discipleship began by awakening to the "myth of equality."[2] In a land like America that prides itself on equality, what do we do when we are faced with the reality of how unequal American experiences and opportunities really are?

SEVEN SYMPTOMS OF SYSTEMIC RACISM

Education is just one area of our society where racism—in the form of racial inequity—is the norm. Racism has been highly adaptive over time, morphing like a monstrous chameleon as its environment has changed. Today, racism works itself out in subtler ways, like systemic racism and the racialization of society; if a society's systems persistently result in different outcomes for different races, you have a **racialized society**.[3]

Let's take a brief look now at seven ways we can know that systemic racism is real.[4]

1. Wealth

Median Wealth per U.S. Family (2019)

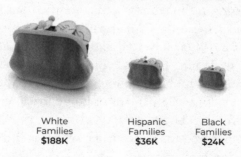

| White Families $188K | Hispanic Families $36K | Black Families $24K |

White families have always been far wealthier than families of color in America. Today, White families enjoy a median net worth that is almost eight times higher than Black families and five times higher than Hispanic families.[5] Even those White workers who don't have a college degree earn more than Black and Hispanic workers who do.[6] Overall, White families hold 90 percent of all the wealth in the country, while Hispanic families hold 2.3 percent and Black families hold 2.6 percent.[7] Can't we spread the love a little more than that?

2. Homeownership

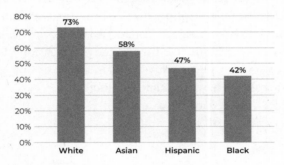

Homeownership Rate by Race

Data Source: Joint Center for Housing Studies (Harvard), 2019

Homeownership is the main way that families can build wealth over time and achieve the "American dream." That's why it's so sad that as of 2019, far fewer families of color owned homes in comparison to White families.[8] Black homeownership, especially, continues to hit all-time lows.[9] Due to a number of discriminatory practices, 98 percent of home loans went to White families between 1934 and 1968.[10] To this day, Blacks are less likely to be approved for a mortgage, which is the type of loan that you need to buy a home.[11]

3. Employment

Black workers are consistently twice as likely to be unemployed as White workers. This has been true for at least sixty years regardless of whether the U.S. economy was going up or down.[12] Black college grads remain twice as likely to be unemployed as other grads.[13] There has also been a massive income gap between Black and White families that has basically remained the same since the 1960s.[14]

Blacks are

2x

more likely to be unemployed

4. Education

More than half of U.S. children are *still* educated in racially concentrated school districts. Why should we be concerned about that? Because separate still does not mean equal. As one study revealed, minority school districts in the United States received $23 billion less in funding than majority ones.[15] You tell me: Do you think they are getting a similar education? Furthermore, students of color are treated differently at school. For example, White students are more likely than Blacks to be identified as gifted, while Black students are three times more likely to be suspended.[16] And why is *that* a big problem? Because, once Black children are in the criminal justice system, they are eighteen times more likely to be sentenced as adults. The problem has gotten so bad that many now refer to the pattern as the **school-to-prison pipeline.**[17]

Minority school districts receive **$23 billion less**

5. Criminal Justice

We all know that America prides itself on being a land of equality and fairness. Yet justice in America is not blind: When a Black person and a White person commit similar crimes, the Black person is more likely to be arrested.[18] Black people are convicted more often and are more likely to receive harsh sentences—in fact, the darker a Black defendant looks, the more likely they are to receive the death penalty![19] And did you know that roughly 70 percent of convicts who have later been proved innocent are people of color?[20] These realities all shed light on why Blacks are incarcerated at five times the rate of Whites. And this **mass incarceration** is a peculiar American phenomenon: Black people comprise 40 percent of the prison population but make up only 13 percent of the U.S. population.[21] What's more, although the United States makes up 5 percent of the global population, it comprises nearly 25 percent of the world's prison population.[22] For whatever reason, we *really* like sending people to jail—especially people of color.

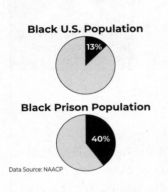

Black U.S. Population

13%

Black Prison Population

40%

Data Source: NAACP

6. Health

The Covid-19 crisis put a spotlight on the existing racial inequities of our healthcare system—the pandemic has been far more devastating for communities of color.[23] People of color are less likely to have access to health insurance; of the thirty million people who remain uninsured in America, about half are people of color.[24] And even when people of color do have access to health insurance, they receive lower-quality care.[25] The most highly trained professionals serve predominantly White communities.[26] Doctors are less likely to order blood tests, CT scans, or X-rays for Black, Latino, and Asian children.[27] When Black patients are admitted to a hospital,

The uninsured are

50%

people of color

they are 1.3 times more likely to die there.[28] The simple verdict, based on the facts? People of color "receive less care—and often worse care—than white Americans."[29]

7. Leadership

Society's leaders are the ones who have the power to make a difference in all the categories we have been exploring. *Yet leaders of color have been severely underrepresented in our halls of power at all points of American history.* In 2020 corporate America, nearly 90 percent of Fortune 500 CEOs were White, and as of 2019, only five Fortune 500 and S&P 500 companies were led by Black CEOs.[30] The pattern in government has been the same. In 2018, for instance, the 116th Congress was the most diverse ever, but only 57 of the 535 voting members of Congress were Black.[31] As of 2020, only two Black governors have ever been elected in the United States, and only six Black senators have  been elected since the Reconstruction.[32] A survey from the same year found that 80 percent of the most powerful people in America were White, even as the United States has become more diverse.[33]

Although we're stopping at seven, we could certainly go on. What we now know is that our society is racialized in countless ways. We are finding persistent inequities in life experiences as wide-ranging as employment, auto loans, mortgage rates, product prices, respect levels, performance expectations, self-esteem, environmental pollution, child poverty, and much more. What do we do with this? I really like this advice: "Let's wake up, for we are no longer the country we think we are."[34]

AWAKENING TO OUR MOMENT

Over time, the concept of awakening has repeatedly been understood as a requirement for racial justice work. In 2017, the term **woke** emerged and won a place in the Merriam-Webster dictionary to mean "aware of and actively attentive to important facts and issues (especially issues of racial and social justice)."[35] *Stay woke* first became a common phrase "in parts of the black community for those who were self-aware, questioning the dominant paradigm and striving for something better."[36] As I'm sure you've heard, the term *woke* has more recently acquired negative connotations, often brandished as a negative term for extreme political correctness. This, however, is a deviation from the original concept.

Nevertheless, the concept of "awakening" to racism is not new—the idea has also been used throughout history to signal a growing consciousness of racial inequity. Did you know that nineteenth-century abolitionists campaigned for President Lincoln under the banner of the "Wide-Awake Club"?

Martin Luther King, Jr., famously urged awakening too:

> One of the great liabilities of history is that all too many people fail to remain awake through great periods of social change. Every society has its protectors of the status quo and its fraternities of the indifferent who are notorious for sleeping through revolutions. But today our very survival depends on our ability to stay awake.[37]

In every generation, followers of Jesus would do well to ask: *Am I snoring my way through a kingdom movement?* Many insist that if they were alive during previous civil rights movements, they would have been on the right side of history. Now is our chance to prove it. We are living through another wave of the Civil

Wide-Awake Club, 1860

Rights Movement, which some have called the "third reconstruction." In the words of Jemar Tisby:

> The *first reconstruction* occurred immediately after the Civil War when newly freed slaves joined in a flowering of Black political, economic, and social participation. The *second reconstruction* happened during the civil rights movement of the 1950s and 1960s when activists assailed the stronghold of Jim Crow segregation. The *third reconstruction* is happening right now. Careful observers agree that the nation is in the midst of another wave of the civil rights movement.[38]

Will this generation awaken to its God-given moment?

I believe that perhaps our most urgent task is for people of all racial backgrounds to get educated about the reality of ongoing racial inequity. If we don't even know about it, there's no way we can fix it! This is how Martin Luther King, Jr., put the need for White people to educate themselves: "Whites, it must frankly be said, are not putting in a similar mass effort to reeducate themselves out of their racial ignorance. It is an aspect of their sense of superiority that the white people of America believe they have so little to learn."[39]

However, please note: Waking up is not for Whites only. I can tell you this from personal experience. People of color like me need awakening too. We live in an age in which many African Americans can and do escape the worst consequences of systemic racism, as I did. Yet while some people of color might be exceptions to the rule, the rule still firmly persists. This explains how it is possible that during the same period in America, we simultaneously elected our first Black president, Barack Obama, *and* experienced a major racial reckoning in Ferguson, Missouri, that helped catalyze the **Black Lives Matter** movement. While a Black president signified progress, Ferguson showed that we still have a long way to go.

2014 FERGUSON PROTESTS

Ferguson is commonly used as shorthand to refer to a series of racial protests that began in Ferguson, Missouri, on August 10, 2014, the day after the fatal shooting of eighteen-year-old Michael Brown by a White police officer. The protests raised debate throughout the world about the relationship between law enforcement officers and African Americans. At the time, America's contradictory racial reality was surprising to many. On the one hand, it seemed that in some ways, Black people in the U.S. had "arrived"—after all, Barack Obama was then leading the country as America's first Black president (2009–2017)! Yet, on the other hand, the events at Ferguson also made it abundantly clear to many that systemic racial inequity is alive and well—and we still have important work to do together.

In the early twentieth century, the activist Marcus Garvey exhorted fellow Blacks to wake up and invest in the uplift of the entire Black community. In the 1972 play *Garvey Lives!,* one of the characters says, "I been sleeping all my life. And now that Mr. Garvey done woke me up, I'm gon' stay woke. And I'm gon' help him wake up other Black folk."[40]

What I have personally discovered is that no one is exempt from the need for awakening.

AWAKENING TO THE SPIRITUAL BATTLE

Although this chapter has been full of facts and statistics, make no mistake: Systemic racism is fundamentally a spiritual sickness. This should not seem so strange to us. The Bible teaches that "our struggle is not against flesh and blood, but against the rulers, against the authorities, against the powers of this dark world and against the spiritual forces of evil in the heavenly realms" (Ephesians 6:12). Other Bible translations use the term *principalities* in this verse. And one way that evil powers and principalities manifest is through broken systems and false ideas.

If we remain blind to the spiritual reality behind systemic racism, we will also remain blind to the spiritual resources available to us.

If we remain blind to the spiritual reality behind systemic racism, we will also remain blind to the spiritual resources available to us. Color-courageous disciples resist the principalities and powers in the same way that Jesus did. Jesus "disarmed [*apekdyomai*] the spiritual rulers and authorities. He shamed them publicly [*deigmatizō*] by his victory over them on the cross" (Colossians

2:15, NLT). The word translated as "disarmed" is *apekdyomai,* which literally means to "take off" or to strip. And "shamed them" translates from *deigmatizō* and means "to expose to public disgrace, to make a spectacle of."[41]

From this, we discover that one of the most effective ways to resist the principalities of systemic racism is simply to *name them.* If you see inequity or unfairness, name it. That's what this chapter has been about—unmasking systemic inequity while simultaneously calling people to dismantle it in Jesus's name. The mere act of exposing systemic racial inequity—bringing it out of darkness and into the light—is key to stripping it of its power.

The mere act of exposing systemic racial inequity—bringing it out of darkness and into the light—is key to stripping it of its power.

Jesus ultimately disarmed the powers and principalities by means of the cross. Once awakened, we, too, can engage in holistic reconciliation—doing evangelism, growing disciples, and stripping systemic injustices like racism of their power—as we abide in Christ and bear our cross together with him.

CHRIST WILL SHINE ON YOU

My all-too-brief experience as a volunteer at an under-resourced school awakened me to reality. It also awakened me to my own need for color-courageous discipleship! I finally saw that while I had access to an excellent public school education because I grew up in a predominantly White community, the reality is that too many Black and Brown youth still do not enjoy that same access.

American disciples cherish the "self-evident" ideal of equality—the bedrock conviction that God created us equal. But it's so important that we don't just cherish *equal creation* at some point in the distant past—let's also strive for *equal opportunity now*. This distinction brings us to the difference between **equality** and **equity**. Equality is about sameness—we all possess the same image of God. Equity is about fairness—we do not all have fair access to opportunity. But it's precisely because all people are created *equal* that all people deserve *equity*.

To be clear, biblical equity is not ultimately about socialism, communism, or any other socioeconomic system. It's about greater fairness in every socioeconomic system. What's more, biblical equity is not about *forcing* equal outcomes. It's about doing what we can to ensure that everyone has a fair shot at life, liberty, and the pursuit of happiness. As we've seen, we still have a long way to go.

Let's not stop at cherishing equal creation
*at some point in the distant past; let's also
strive for* equal opportunity now.

I love the Ignatian concept of **magis,** which in Latin means "more." The Ignatians (Society of Jesus) are an ancient religious order of Catholic monks, and they have long used the concept of *magis* as a reminder that Jesus continually invites disciples to *more*—to see Christ more clearly and abide in Christ more deeply so that we might bear Christ's fruit more abundantly. Jesus says to the church: "Wake up, and strengthen what remains and is about to die, for I have not found your works complete in the sight of my God" (Revelation 3:2, ESV). Over time, I have been awakening to the ways in which my own deeds have been *good* but *incomplete*. Perhaps you, too, are starting to awaken. Once you *do* begin to awaken, you might wonder: *Wow, these problems are so big. What can I really do about them?* Believe me, many adults feel that way too! But don't get overwhelmed. For now, the most important thing you can do is *continue to wake up,* continue to grow in awareness. Make a decision that you will not miss out on the fullness of the kingdom of God! You still have your whole life ahead of you to make a difference.

And, in the end, the disciple's reward for waking up is more of Jesus Christ: "Wake up, sleeper, rise from the dead, and Christ will shine on you" (Ephesians 5:14). Some believe that early disciples sang this as a hymn of repentance to move from being passive partners of darkness to active agents of light. So, it is delightfully good news to discover that in the end, the disciple's reward for waking up is *more of Jesus Christ.*

Just as he did with his disciples in the Garden of Gethsemane, Jesus is now nudging you to awaken from your slumber. And as you continue to awaken, you will find that you'll experience *more:* more opportunities to courageously transform the world and more of the glory of God.

THINK ABOUT IT

1. When have you experienced some kind of awakening in your own discipleship journey, whether or not related to race?

2. Why do you think the Bible most often urges believers (rather than unbelievers) to "wake up"?

3. Explain in your own words what the "myth of equality" is all about.

4. Review again the list of seven ways we know systemic racism is true. Which one(s) stand out to you most and why?

5. Share what this verse means to you personally: "Wake up, sleeper, rise from the dead, and Christ will shine on you" (Ephesians 5:14).

DISCIPLESHIP AS WARDROBE CHANGE

Take Off the Bias That Holds You Back

> The ancient world, just like the modern, was an elaborate
> network of prejudice . . . so ingrained as to be thought
> normal and natural.
>
> —N. T. WRIGHT, *COLOSSIANS AND PHILEMON*

Whenever we begin a new discipleship journey, I think that we tend to envision ourselves as a *tabula rasa*—a "blank slate," as the Greek philosopher Aristotle put it. We like to think that we begin new learning experiences with a neutral mindset: objective, clear-eyed, and level-headed. Unfortunately, though, this blank slate idea is more pagan than Christian!

Our human nature has been stained by sin from the start. What's more, over time, our minds are further shaped by the sinful patterns of a broken world. That's why the Scriptures insist: "Do not conform to the pattern of this world, but be transformed by the renewing of your mind" (Romans 12:2).

In the category of race, what does it mean to renew our minds? I am convinced that one important way to renew our minds is to uproot **unconscious bias** (also known as **implicit bias**). It seems that a huge gap stubbornly persists between our *intentions* and the actual *impact* that we are having on the world.

I call this the **intention vs. impact dilemma.** Somehow, people just like you and me who have the best of intentions when it comes to race are *still* fostering racial inequity. How can this be?

Unpacking unconscious bias can help us understand our confounding racial contradictions. We are all inclined toward unconscious bias, regardless of our racial background. In fact, it's quite common for people of color to experience unconscious bias even toward their own racial group—which I discovered, to my astonishment, was true of me.

---

*People who have the best of intentions when it comes to race is **still** fostering racial inequity. How can this be?*

I serve as a leader for the Evangelical Covenant Church (ECC), a denominational network of churches known for its multiethnic commitment. One of my most treasured Covenant experiences has been the Journey to Mosaic (J2M). It is a bus tour that travels to sites of civil rights significance in America for multiple racial and ethnic groups.

When I went on the Journey to Mosaic, our first stop was the Nisei Veterans Memorial Hall in Seattle. Did you know that during World War II, Japanese people in America were forced to leave their homes and enter into internment camps? We had the chance to hear the story of an older Japanese woman who actually experienced one of these camps. Or did you know that Chinese people were once suddenly banned from entering our country? This was due to the **Chinese Exclusion Act,** which I had never even heard of before I visited the Chinese Reconciliation Park in Tacoma. I will also never forget my first visit to a Native American reservation, the Yakama Nation. Although there are over three hundred Native American reservations in the United States, my guess is that most Americans have never visited one—which is a massive missed opportunity for us to connect and grow. During my own visit to the Yakama Nation, we stood at an unmarked burial ground and remembered the Native American people who died as they resisted the Europeans who forcibly took their land.

The Chinese Must Go! poster, 1885

But my most pivotal moment occurred during our final session. Someone started talking about racial inequity in Black communities, and I began to automatically experience cringeworthy thoughts like these: *Well, I wish it weren't true, but Black communities are plagued with Black-on-Black crime. Broken communities are the sad but obvious result. It's our own fault.* I am embarrassed to admit these now. I kept most of these thoughts to myself at the time, but in the group conversation that followed, some of these very ideas were addressed head-on—and unmasked as both unhelpful and misleading.

That night, I began to realize the depths of my own unconscious bias—*toward my own community*—for the first time. The Lord placed a mirror before me: Although I thought I was "looking good" as I interacted with others, I was actually clothed with the dirty rags of unconscious bias. In fact, my bias had a name: attribution error. **Attribution error** causes people to give out blame in lopsided ways. It causes us to look at a suffering person and blame the person rather than also taking that person's circumstances into account. Because of attribution error, our human tendency is to blame the victim and overlook any possible victimizers; to blame the oppressed and overlook the oppressive circumstances; to blame a community's "culture" and overlook the community's history and the injustices inflicted upon it.

Let's continue with the specific example of attribution error. When looking at a predominantly Black community riddled with poverty and crime, some people might quietly think thoughts like: *Black people must not be as smart or hardworking as others. The fact that Black people are more criminal than others is sad but true. I wonder what it is about Black culture that keeps them in the gutter. Of course, there are exceptions . . . but in general, these people need to get their act together.* Very few people would say these things out loud, but some still think them. In fact, it is a tragic thing indeed that both non-Black people *and even some Black people* can have thoughts like these due to the biased ways in which we have all been conditioned. Yet all these ideas are symptoms of our underlying attribution error. They are completely lacking in compassion and real, comprehensive understanding. What's more, they do very little to get at the root causes of our society's challenges so that we can find effective solutions together.

Color-courageous disciples of all races and backgrounds strive to be different. They do this by asking more helpful questions: *What is leading to such high levels of crime and despair? How might the system itself be failing this community, even unintentionally? What resources are needed here for empowerment, growth, and healing? When it comes to crime, what would it look like to have an attitude of restoration rather than punishment? For that matter, are these citizens being fairly convicted and sentenced to begin with? Why don't more people care about questions like these? And how can I be part of the solution?*

Now, listen: I am certainly not arguing that individuals or communities should never take responsibility for their own actions. What I am calling for—and, more important, what the Scriptures seem to call for—is that disciples of Christ demonstrate both truth *and* amazing grace rather than pharisaical, cold-hearted judgment.

If we look, we'll see that the Bible addresses unconscious bias too—albeit in different terms. In the story of the man born blind, for example, the disciples reveal their judgmental attitude when they ask Jesus: "Who sinned, this man or his parents, that he was born blind?" Jesus bluntly rebukes them for this question, saying: "Neither this man nor his parents sinned . . . but this happened so that the works of God might be displayed in him. As long as it is day, we must do the works of him who sent me" (John 9:2–4).

Jesus does two intriguing things with this response. First, he pushes back on the disciples' attribution error, rebuking their knee-jerk reaction to blame the victim. Second, he challenges them to get to work. As disciples, when we see a person or a community suffering, it's not time to play the blame game. It is time for us to wake up, collaborate with God, and get to work.

Well, you might think, *maybe this blind man didn't sin, but what about people who clearly do sin? Don't they deserve blame?* Good question. For that, let's take a look at the Bible story of the woman caught in adultery. Even in this story—where the woman clearly *has* done something wrong—Jesus's response is beautifully balanced (John 8:1–11). Did this woman deserve death according to Jewish law? Yes, she did (Deuteronomy 22:22). Nevertheless, Jesus does a curious thing: He draws attention not to this woman's *obvious sin* but rather to her accusers' *hidden sin*— their judgmentalism, hypocrisy, and pride. Jesus does acknowledge the woman's sin and tells her to sin no more. But he refuses to condemn her with words like *You messed up and now you get to suffer the consequences!* No, his attitude is one of restoration. Jesus gently and graciously seeks to help her and restore her to the community.

When it comes to race, we are called not to *be conformed* to the pattern of this world, which is inclined to condemn and abandon broken people, including ourselves. We are called instead to *be transformed* by the renewing of our minds and to help build beloved community.

CALLED TO WARDROBE CHANGE

Jesus launched his preaching ministry with a dual call: "'The time has come,' he said. 'The kingdom of God has come near. Repent and believe the good news!'" (Mark 1:15). Jesus here names two distinct actions that he requires of disciples: The first is to *turn away* from former ways (repent). Only then can we *turn toward* Jesus (believe), which is the second action. These two simple actions—repent and believe—are the basis for all ongoing discipleship and transformation in Christ.

I mentioned earlier that the Bible does not utilize "blank slate" metaphors when it comes to spiritual growth. Instead, we see curious metaphors like a wardrobe change! Before the Lord, even our best deeds are filthy garments (Isaiah 64:6). Growing as a disciple, then, involves a dual process of wardrobe change: *taking off our filthy garments*—including our distorted mindsets—and *putting on the way of Christ.* And here's the thing: The Scriptures reveal that wardrobe change is particularly relevant when it comes to our mindsets about ethnicity:

> You have taken off your old self with its practices and have put on the new self. . . . *Here there is no Gentile or Jew, circumcised or uncircumcised, barbarian, Scythian, slave or free, but Christ is all, and is in all.* Therefore, as God's chosen people, holy and dearly loved, clothe yourselves with compassion, kindness, humility,

gentleness and patience. . . . And over all these virtues put on love. (Colossians 3:9–12, 14)

Here's another way of saying it: Left to your own devices, dear disciples, your default will be to mistreat people who are different from you, whether you realize it or not. Seek to identify the world's biased mindsets in yourself so that you can take those rags off and clothe yourself instead with the mindset of Christ.

Before the Lord, even our best deeds are like dirty clothes—we need to take those rags off and put on something new. When the Bible describes spiritual growth, it uses metaphors like *wardrobe change*. Growing as a disciple involves continually taking off our dirty clothes and putting on Christ. The "dirty clothes" that we need to take off include natural, sinful tendencies, distorted worldviews, and more. In the same way, color-courageous disciples work to intentionally discover and take off the rags of worldly racial mindsets, then put on the fresh robes of the new. You can't have one without the other.

SEVEN CATEGORIES OF UNCONSCIOUS BIAS

We have already mentioned how we have all been unconsciously "discipled" by the powerful racial narratives of the world. That is why, in the words of my friend David Swanson, we need to be rediscipled—especially with regard to our minds.[1] As we learned in chapter 2, theologians refer to the impact of sin on our minds as **the noetic effect of sin,** which means that even our ability to process information accurately has been compromised by sin. Did you know that a full 98 percent of what our brain does, it does *without* our conscious awareness?[2] It's our unconscious racial attitudes—in other words, our unconscious biases—that really help to shed light on our bewildering racial contradictions.

Unconscious bias is another term for **cognitive bias;** both refer to a habitual misperception of the mind. We now know that human cognitive biases fall into well-worn patterns. Just as we looked in the previous chapter at seven symptoms of systemic racism, so now we will look at seven categories of unconscious bias as well as practical ideas for "taking off" each one.

1. Pro-White Preference

It seems that most people today, including young children, unconsciously have a *pro-White, anti-Black bias.*[3] For example, a significant majority of Whites, Asian Americans, and Latinos showed anti-Black bias when given a special test that measures bias. And here's the crazy thing: Almost half of African Americans show anti-Black bias too![4] Want to hear an example of how pro-White bias plays out in real life? Here's a college example: Thousands of college professors

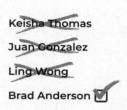

were sent an email from a fake student asking for an appointment to discuss their school's programs. The emails were identical *except for the names of the students*—which varied by perceived ethnicity. And guess what? "Professors were *more responsive to White male students* than to female, Black, Hispanic, Indian or Chinese students in almost every discipline and across all types of universities."[5] What we learn is that simply having the "wrong" name was enough for a professor to treat a potential student unfairly! Did they do this intentionally? In most cases, I doubt it. That's why we call pro-White preference an *unconscious* bias.

Take Off the Dirty Rags: *Before you make any judgments about a person, especially if you don't know them well, stop and think: How might pro-White, anti-Black preference be unconsciously impacting your judgment?*

2. Blame

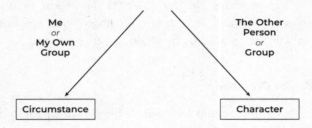

Where Should We Place Blame?

When we encounter a problematic situation, we understandably want to figure out who is to blame. Unfortunately, as I mentioned in my experience with attribution error, we tend to answer the blame question in a biased way. For example, when a person is cut off while driving, she might assume that the offender did so because they are a horrible person ("What a jerk!")—not because they are in the middle of some horrible circumstance ("This driver must be responding to an emergency"). Color-courageous disciples strive to take a more balanced approach, keeping in mind a person's *circumstances* as well as any relevant concerns about a person's *character*. Disciples are commanded not to judge for the obvious reason that our human interpretation of a person's actions can never be as comprehensive as God's (Matthew 7:1–5). Actually, God calls us to be biased . . . not toward blame, but toward grace.

Take Off the Dirty Rags: *When you encounter someone doing something negative, do not assume something is wrong with a person's entire group or culture. Take a step back and consider: How might this person's circumstances or community history be influencing their behavior?*

3. Dehumanization

Did you know that we have a tendency toward **dehumanization**—to believe that those outside our group are somehow *less human* than we are? It's a ridiculous idea, but research has shown it to be very true.[6] And what's the problem with assuming that someone is less human? The problem is that once that happens, it becomes easier to mistreat them. In her book *Biased,* Jennifer Eberhardt writes:

"I Am a Man," diorama of Memphis Sanitation Workers Strike, National Civil Rights Museum, Downtown Memphis, Tennessee*

PHOTO BY ADAM JONES, PhD

> Marginalized groups in countries all over the world are often discredited through animal imagery. Disfavored immigrant groups—Mexicans in the United States, Jews in Germany, the Roma in Italy, Muslims across the European continent—are frequently likened to insects, rodents, and other vermin. . . . [It's] been a universal fixture of human history.[7]

Isn't that sad? In the United States, the dehumanization of African Americans has been an especially peculiar problem. The problem started long ago—after all, it was way easier to enslave and discriminate against Black people if they were understood to be more like beasts than human beings. Unfortunately, this isn't just a relic of the past. Did you know that as recently as 2016, police officers in San Francisco referred to Black people in their

★   https://commons.wikimedia.org/w/index.php?title=File:I_Am_a _Man_-_Diorama_of_Memphis_Sanitation_Workers_Strike_-_National _Civil_Rights_Museum_-_Downtown_Memphis_-_Tennessee_-_USA .jpg&oldid=491566088

text messages as "wild animals, cockroaches, savages, barbarians, and monkeys"?[8] The results of this are tragic: When police officers associate young Black males with apes, they are more likely to use excessive force against them.[9] The big takeaway here is this: To the extent that society believes a racial group to be less than human—*even if subtly*—that society is prone to feel less compassion *and* to tolerate greater violence against that group.

Because all people are created in God's image, we must strive to resist even the subtlest forms of dehumanization. I believe this was the heart of what Jesus taught when he said: "Anyone who says to a brother or sister, 'Raca,' is answerable to the court. And anyone who says, 'You fool!' will be in danger of the fire of hell" (Matthew 5:22). These terms—*raca* and *fool*—are code for the dehumanization that happens so easily in the human heart.

Take Off the Dirty Rags: *Take off the tendency to dehumanize whole groups in both big and little ways—not just publicly but in your own heart. Make it your goal to understand what you have in common with others.*

4. Criminalization

VS.

Black boys are suspended **3X** more than White boys

Racial profiling happens when someone is suspected of wrongdoing primarily based on their race. Did you know that in school, Black children are perceived to be less innocent and more mature than what would be natural for their age?[10] This actually leads administrators and teachers to suspend and discipline Black children at higher rates, which reinforces the school-to-prison pipeline that we talked about.[11] And in the community, police associate darker skin more strongly with crime. One reason for this may be that Black people are *overrepresented* as violent criminals in the news when compared to actual arrest rates.[12] At the same time, they are chronically *underrepresented* as positive role models in the media.[13] What do you think the impact of that would be?

Take Off the Dirty Rags: *Be sure to notice when people of color are portrayed in books and movies in negative ways, and consider what that implies. Notice and seek out resources where people of color are portrayed in positive ways.*

5. Stereotype Threat

Stereotype threat is what happens when negative stereotypes impact a person's performance. This is really a crazy situation: It means that if you're worried that someone's negative beliefs about you are right, then you are actually *more likely* to prove those negative beliefs to be true—because you are so worried about doing that! For example, Black students performed more poorly on standardized tests when their race was emphasized. When race was *not* emphasized, however, Black students performed just as well as White students. What we have learned is that "performance . . . can be harmed simply by the awareness that one's behavior might be [negatively] viewed through the lens of racial stereotypes."[14]

Take Off the Dirty Rags: *Realize that other people's expectations for your group (being a person of color, being female, even being young!) can impact how you perform—if you let it. Resist those stereotypes and remember you are an individual person, and your success is ultimately up to you!*

6. Status Quo Bias

The *status quo* refers to things as they are, right now. Humans have a natural tendency to resist changes to the status quo—even when those changes are shown to be beneficial. Weirdly, both

Back to Egypt, please!

the powerful and the less powerful members of society are prone to defend the status quo. While the advantaged group has a clear interest in preserving the status quo, the disadvantaged group is actually interested in minimizing any further losses that might come with change—even good change.[15] Regardless of where we find ourselves on the social scale, we humans prefer stability to change, which is why we find ways to rationalize and defend the way things are. Consider the Israelites: Despite their miraculous deliverance from slavery in Egypt, they pined after their former life when faced with new challenges and conspired to find a way back (Exodus 16:3; Numbers 14:4)! That's what **status quo bias** does, and it's one reason that it's so hard to change the racial status quo of our society.

Take Off the Dirty Rags: *When you are challenged to change in some way, remember that your natural response will be to resist. Strive to be open to new ways of doing things or seeing the world, especially when it comes to race.*

7. Truth Distortion

There are many other ways in which our minds distort the truth. Too many to name here, in fact. Here are just three: (1) Our **bias blind spot** means that even if we know we are biased, we will *still* tend to see ourselves as less biased than other people! (2) We see what we *want* to believe, even if it's false (that's called **confirmation bias**). (3) We avoid unpleasant information, even if it's true (that's called the **ostrich effect**).[16] The implications of all this should be clear: At the end of the day, color-courageous

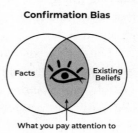

Confirmation Bias

Facts

Existing Beliefs

What you pay attention to

disciples should embrace humility as a way of life—as long as we have breath, we will *always* need God's help to overcome our biases.

Take Off the Dirty Rags: *Remember: Even after learning all of this, you will still assume that you are less biased than other people! The only "cure" for our bias is to put on the humility of Jesus. Proactively seek out feedback, especially from those who are different from you. Always resist the temptation to believe that you have "arrived." Don't get defensive— be willing to listen, learn, and confess blind spots as others point them out to you.*

Unfortunately, these seven categories of unconscious bias are just the beginning! In considering that, I find myself drawn back to Paul's agonized words in Romans: "I decide to do good, but I don't *really* do it; I decide not to do bad, but then I do it anyway. . . . Something has gone wrong deep within me and gets the better of me every time" (7:17–20, MSG).

Our bias is unconscious, but that does not mean that it is altogether undetectable or unchangeable.

Remember: Wardrobe change is a lifelong discipleship process. Although we may never root out our unconscious bias completely, we *can* continue to learn more about human bias so that we might not be ruled by it. Our bias is unconscious, but that does not mean that it is altogether undetectable or unchangeable.

This survey of unconscious bias should reinforce just how much we need to embrace Christlike humility. Color-courageous disciples must be the type of people who exemplify humility. It takes courage to admit that we are imperfect and always will be. With racism—as with so many other challenges—the change must start with us.

FROM COLOR-BLIND TO COLOR-BRAVE

There's one more racial mindset that we need to address: the mindset of **color blindness.** Many have wondered: Can't we just be color-blind? Color-blind people say: "I don't see color." They counsel others: "Try not to notice the color of people's skin. That way, you can steer clear of bias." They quote Martin Luther King, Jr.'s "I Have a Dream" speech: "I have a dream that my four children will one day live in a nation where they will not be judged by the color of their skin, but by the content of their character." We'll return to King's words shortly, but first, a few reflections on why color blindness doesn't work. Actually, it's a dirty rag that must be taken off too!

Most who embrace color blindness do so with the best of intentions. They acknowledge that racism is a problem, and they see color blindness as a solution. I think we can all agree that we'd rather not be judged based on the color of our skin! However, when taken too far, color blindness also has unintended consequences.

First, color blindness minimizes both race *and* ethnicity. It is true that *race* has been a harmful human construct—but, as we know, *ethnicity* is a God-given gift. Those who say that they "don't see color" are prone to miss out on the valuable contributions of ethnic diversity.

Second, it's actually a moot point because it's impossible to succeed at being color-blind anyway. We see color whether we consciously want to or not. That's what this whole chapter has been about! We all have unconscious racial perspectives that distort our judgment. The reality, as we have seen, is that we are *not* blank slates. We have already been deeply formed by our society's racial values, whether we realize it or not. As much as we might like to say that race doesn't matter, our brains behave otherwise. That is why the most effective response to race and racism is not denial, nonaction, or "blindness"—but rather, intentional color-courageous discipleship.

> **As much as we might like to say that race doesn't matter, our brains behave otherwise.**

Finally, and most importantly, color blindness ironically leads to racial inequity—precisely the *opposite* of what is intended![17] Why is that? Because *those who do not see race also cannot see racism.*

Those who resist racial realities are liable to remain naively unaware of their own racial biases. Those who prefer not to countenance racial categories are often responsible for suppressing the critical conversations that we need to have about race in order to make real progress.

Color blindness ironically leads to racial inequity—
precisely the opposite of what is intended.

In *The Psychology of Racial Colorblindness,* Philip J. Mazzocco summarizes the research on color blindness. His surprising conclusion: The consequences of color blindness appear to be almost entirely negative![18] This is why we need to move from being color-blind to being **color-courageous.**[19] Color-courageous disciples choose to see color for the sake of cultivating racial equity. When we choose to be color-courageous, we can more easily see the racial disparities before us. We can become attentive to our own biases. We can listen to one another's racial stories. And we can seek solutions together.

Returning to Martin Luther King, Jr.'s famous quote: To deduce that King was color-blind on the basis of one sentence from one speech is to take his words out of context. When we review the entire scope of his life and work, we will discover that *King was not color-blind but color-courageous.*

Incidentally, Jesus himself was not color-blind. He was color-courageous. After all, he charged us with a strikingly colorful commission to make disciples of all cultures and ethnicities—which, of course, color-blind disciplemakers could never fulfill (Matthew 28:19–21)!

Putting On the Mind of Christ

Clotho Among the Three Fates

Did you know that *clothing* has long been a metaphor for *life*? In Greek mythology, for example, the goddess Clotho was one of the three Fates who determined the course of a life. Every individual life was a thread. Clotho spun the thread, Lachesis drew it out, and Atropos cut the thread upon one's death.

We have seen that in the Scriptures, too, clothing is used as a metaphor for life. That's why, if you want to change your life, you've got to change your clothes! In the Old Testament, we see this illustrated in the life of the high priest Joshua: His spiritual transformation was depicted through a wardrobe change as the angels exchanged his filthy garments of sin for robes of righteousness (Zechariah 3:4).

In the New Testament, wardrobe change is especially applied to the disciples' need to transform the way they engage the ethnic "other"—Jew or Gentile, circumcised or uncircumcised, barbarian, and even Scythian, a people understood at the time to be the worst of the worst, savages, the so-called dregs of society.

Now, after learning about unconscious bias, perhaps you are wondering: *If bias is unconscious, is taking it off even possible?* Thankfully, studies have shown that it is, and we've touched upon some of the ways of doing so in this chapter.[20] But even beyond the solutions that the world provides to uproot unconscious bias, disciples have something more. In the New Testament, the righteous robe that God clothes us with is Jesus himself: "For all of you who were baptized into Christ have clothed yourselves with Christ" (Galatians 3:27).

On my own journey with unconscious bias, I have come to understand at a gut level that putting on Christ looks like putting on a courageous mindset of Christlike humility (Colossians 3:12). The Greek word for repent, *metanoeō,* derives from *meta-* ("to change") and *-noeō* ("the mind"). To repent means to change our minds to be like Christ's—and *humility* is exactly how the Bible describes the mind of Jesus:

> In your relationships with one another, *have the same mindset as Christ Jesus:*

> Who, being in very nature God,
>   did not consider equality with God something to be used to
>   his own advantage;
> rather, he made himself nothing
>   by taking the very nature of a servant,
>   being made in human likeness.
> And being found in appearance as a man,
>   *he humbled himself*
>   by becoming obedient to death—
>   even death on a cross! (Philippians 2:5–8)

Friend, how do we "overcome" unconscious bias? The only way is through Christlike humility. Bias is—and always will be—a challenge for every single one of us. Putting on Christlike humility means coming to terms with this. It means accepting that our intentions simply will not always line up with our impact. It means forever resisting the temptation to say that we have "arrived." But most of all, putting on Christlike humility means making the courageous choice to repent and believe for a lifetime—which is the very heart of what discipleship is all about.

THINK ABOUT IT

1. In your own words, what does it mean to "repent and believe"? When have you done this in your own life?

2. What are some racial mindsets you would like to take off? What would you like to put on instead?

3. Take a look again at the list of seven categories of unconscious bias. Which one(s) stand out to you and why?

4. In your own words, how would you describe why color blindness can be problematic? What does it mean to move from "color-blind" to "color-courageous"?

5. Why do you think it's so hard for us to put on the humble mindset of Jesus Christ? What would that look like for you now?

DISCIPLESHIP AS INNER HEALING

Be Healed Before You Heal the World

Only through an inner spiritual transformation do we
gain the strength to fight vigorously the evils of the world
in a humble and loving spirit.

—MARTIN LUTHER KING, JR., *STRENGTH TO LOVE*

The town of Capernaum is a frenzy of enthusiasm—Jesus is home! It is now common knowledge that this is no run-of-the-mill rabbi. This Jesus can *do miracles.* Word is spreading like rushing lava that "the Lord's healing power [is] strongly with Jesus" (Luke 5:17, NLT).

Today we have a front-row seat to the rabbi—a miracle itself as the "house . . . [is] so packed with visitors that there [is] no more room, even outside the door" (Mark 2:2, NLT). Along with the crowd, we are enchanted by the rabbi's teaching.

Suddenly, shouts and commotion from overhead—the roof is caving in! We take cover but then crane our necks to observe that the roof is not *caving in* but *opening up.* A rectangle of sunshine bursts open, and a shaft of light streams down. In a shower of straw and debris, a paralyzed man is descending like a heap of cargo, landing flush before Jesus. Unprecedented. All eyes are on the rabbi. How will he respond?

He responds, as usual, in a surprising way. Jesus is not bothered; he is beaming. He opens his mouth with words of healing, but they are certainly not the words we are expecting. "Be encouraged, my child!" Jesus declares with elation. "Your sins are forgiven" (Matthew 9:2, NLT).

Wait—what? Instead of healing the man, Jesus perplexes everyone with talk of forgiveness. But shortly thereafter, in a flurry of further excitement and confusion, Jesus *does* heal the man's paralysis too. But he does it almost as an afterthought. With the crowd, we gaze upon the strange rabbi in wonder, and the eyes of our hearts open to a peculiar idea: Perhaps physical healing isn't Jesus's primary concern.

Healing the Paralytic at Capernaum engraving by Bernhard Rode, 1780

For Jesus, tangible miracles are merely signs pointing to subtler yet more significant miracles. Today, we are too often just like the paralyzed man and his friends: We respectfully demand that Jesus stop whatever he's doing so he can get to the more urgent business of healing our more "obvious" problems! But Jesus yearns for us to experience a far deeper kind of healing.

> *Jesus seeks to heal and liberate us from sin, guilt, and shame so that we can transform the world in God's way.*

Together we have taken a hard look at the vast racial brokenness of our world. Seeing this, color-courageous disciples are rightly eager to go about the business of dismantling racism and making a difference. That agenda is good, but Jesus's agenda is fuller and better. Jesus wants to see racism dismantled, but he also wants to liberate us from sin, guilt, and shame. Jesus seeks to bring about the kind of inner transformation we need to transform our world in God's way.

NAMING OUR TRAUMA

My husband and I went to seminary together. Seminary is the kind of graduate school you need to go to if you want to become a pastor. Well, we went to seminary with bright ambitions to change the world for God. Little did we know that God's ambition was different. God's ambition was—and still is—to change us!

For example, at the end of a certain semester, when the Boston chill was beginning to bite the air, I should've been thrilled because I had just handed in my final paper. Instead, I was lying on my couch in the fetal position, rocking back and forth in the dark.

I had begun to experience severe bouts of panic, depression, and anxiety. I became enraged whenever I felt disappointed in my relationships. I was plagued with anxiety when I feared I was not making the best career decisions and was tortured by panic when I felt that I hadn't done something *just right*. That night, I was paralyzed with terror that I had just submitted a paper . . . that wasn't perfect.

Eventually, I came across Richard Winter's *Perfecting Ourselves to Death*. What a title, right? Well, I recognized myself on nearly every page. As I began to unearth the dysfunctional depths of perfectionism in my life, God helped me see how racial trauma had played a major role. As a Black girl, I grew up believing the lie that I was a member of the lowest rung of society. I came to believe that I couldn't just perform *as well as* others. I had to do *twice as well* as others if I hoped to earn the exact same rewards. In time, I fully embraced the false narrative that as a Black girl, I must not—could not—ever tolerate imperfection. I didn't fully realize it at the time, but this is a form of trauma. **Trauma** comes from the Greek word for "wound." I began to experience deep healing as I was able to name my wounds and seek healing. In the same way, color-courageous disciples can increasingly defang racism as we grow in our capacity to *name* the specific trauma that racism has caused, both in ourselves and in others.

My original vision for this book did not include a chapter on healing. But then I came to realize that in a traumatized world, healing, discipleship, and building beloved community are all intimately intertwined. What's more, as color-courageous disciples, we will be effective in God's mission to make the world whole only to the extent that we are whole ourselves—spiritually, emotionally, relationally, and in every other way.

In a traumatized world, healing, discipleship, and mission are all intimately intertwined.

In addition to grappling with the racial trauma of people of color, though, color-courageous disciples would do well to unpack the surprising truth that racism traumatizes both victims and victimizers. As it turns out, White people have been traumatized by racism too—it just takes a different form. Let's take a look at what trauma looks like in more depth for both groups, beginning with people of color.

RACIAL TRAUMA IN PEOPLE OF COLOR

In her book *Healing Racial Trauma,* Sheila Wise Rowe describes the dizzying array of trauma that racism inflicts upon people of color. *Trauma* refers to the spiritual, emotional, and relational wounds that linger and continue to cause pain after a distressing event. Of course, racism has *not* impacted all people of color in the same way. Personally, I can relate to some forms of racial trauma but not others. Yet color-courageous disciples also seek to understand the racial trauma that *others* have experienced in order to build a mutually healing beloved community. Let's take a look now at three categories of racial trauma: *individual, corporate,* and *divine.*

Individual Racial Trauma

Did you know that *physical* **hate crimes** toward individuals are still quite common? In fact, hate crime incidents rose in 2019 to levels not seen in a decade.[1] In 2020, the FBI revealed that of all the hate crimes committed, the vast majority (61 percent) were motivated by racial bias.[2] In schools, more than one-third of adolescents who report bullying experience *bias-based* bullying—which is actually *more* strongly associated with diminished health than general bullying.[3]

Emotional wounds, while "invisible," still inflict real damage. For example, "students who experience bullying are at increased risk for depression, anxiety, sleep difficulties, lower academic achievement, and dropping out of school."[4]

Even just *witnessing* someone else's distress can result in trauma. This is called **vicarious trauma.** If you experience something vicariously, it means that you experience it *through* someone else as you observe or hear about their experiences. For example, after racially charged incidents with the police, individuals throughout a Black community have a heightened stress response for some time.[5]

Corporate Racial Trauma

It is good that there has been a widespread awakening to systemic racism. But to make real progress toward healing, we also need a widespread awakening to the reality of *systemic trauma*— the corporate trauma caused by systemic racism.

An example: A Native American social worker by the name of Maria Yellow Horse Brave Heart devoted herself to understanding why entire communities of Indigenous peoples have languished over generations.[6] She coined the diagnosis of **historical racial trauma,** the "collective emotional and psychological injury both over the life span and across generations."[7] The repercussions of historical racial trauma include mental illness, family dysfunction, alcohol abuse, and even premature mortality. Similar historical racial trauma can also be observed among Black communities (dubbed "post-traumatic slave syndrome"), Japanese Americans (after the internment camps of World War II), and Jewish communities (after the Holocaust).[8]

Just as there has been a widespread awakening to the reality of systemic racism, so too do we need a similar awakening to the reality of systemic trauma.

Recent studies on the impact of the Jewish Holocaust across generations have yielded a further discovery called **transgenerational racial trauma**—trauma that is, astonishingly, passed down genetically.[9] We now know this:

Trauma can alter the DNA expression of a child or grandchild's brain, causing a wide range of . . . health issues, including memory loss, chronic anxiety, muscle weakness, and depression. Some of these effects seem particularly prevalent among African Americans, Jews, and American Indians, three groups who have experienced an enormous amount of historical trauma.[10]

A 2015 study of Jewish Holocaust survivors "demonstrated that damaged genes in the bodies of Jewish Holocaust survivors . . . were passed on to their children."[11] In fact, a new field of scientific inquiry, **epigenetics,** has now emerged to study inherited changes in gene expression.[12]

Finally, a third type of corporate trauma is environmental racial trauma. This is trauma caused by **environmental racism,** which happens when communities of color are disproportionately exposed to pollutants. The Flint water crisis is a prime example. Here's another example: Did you know that there is widespread inequality when it comes to the locations of hazardous waste facilities?[13] This means that if you are a person of color, you are far more likely to live by a dangerous garbage dump. How unfair is that?

FLINT WATER CRISIS

The Flint water crisis was a public health crisis that took place in Flint, Michigan, from 2014 to 2019. Residents of Flint—a predominantly African American community—had been complaining about the taste, smell, and color of their drinking water for over a year. People were shocked to discover that Flint's drinking water had been strongly contaminated with lead. This happened after officials switched the city's water source to the Flint River to save money. Tragically, over one hundred thousand residents were exposed to elevated lead levels, including six thousand to twelve thousand children. This is devastating: Long-term lead poisoning has real consequences, including pain, fatigue, anemia, and brain damage.

Divine Racial Trauma

All trauma is harmful, but perhaps the most destructive kind is **divine racial trauma,** trauma that negatively impacts our relationship with God. Obviously, our God does not traumatize us, but it sure can seem that way. Why, for instance, does God allow racism and oppression to thrive, bullies to taunt, inequity to continue? Why has God allowed slavery and other racial atrocities to flourish for so long, especially in a "Christian" country? Questions like these are what weaken the faith of some and cause many others to reject the Christian faith outright.

Let's take the life of Malcolm X as a case in point. He was raised in a Christian family by a father who served as a preacher. But in addition to preaching the gospel, Malcolm's father also taught Black people to be proud of who they were. Unfortunately, as Malcolm recounted, the "good Christian white people" in the neighborhood weren't happy about that.[14] While Malcolm's mother was pregnant with him, the Ku Klux Klan arrived at their home, brandishing torches, rifles, and threats. Later, Malcolm's earliest memory was seeing his house burn to the ground while White police and firemen stood by and watched.[15] Can you imagine?

Soon after, Malcolm's father was murdered. His body was found laid across train tracks, his head smashed in, and his body severed nearly in half. Although the family had purchased life insurance in case of such a tragedy, local authorities denied the family's claim. Over time, Malcolm's family became destitute, and his mother was committed to an asylum. While he had always had doubts, Malcolm eventually rejected his father's faith once and for all. When Malcolm X did return to faith in time, it was not to Christianity but to a religion called the Nation of

Islam. In this movement, Malcolm found a religion that addressed the evils of racism against Black people forcefully and directly—as his experience of Christianity never had.

When I think of Malcolm X's rejection of the God of Jesus Christ, my heart aches. His story is exhibit A for divine racial trauma, but there are many others who have a story like his. Still more have held on to the Christian faith, but their relationship with God has suffered real damage due to the divine racial trauma they have experienced.

APPLES, BANANAS, AND COCONUTS: THE ABCS OF INTERNALIZED RACISM

Let's look at one more example of racial trauma for people of color: **internalized racism.** This is what happens when marginalized racial groups internalize society's negative narratives about themselves.

The 1947 Doll Test

One of the clearest demonstrations of internalized racism was the famed doll test. In this social psychology test of 1947, Black children were presented with two dolls—one Black and one White. They were asked which doll they wanted to play with and to identify which doll was the "nice" one and which was the "bad" one. A majority of the Black children preferred the White dolls and shunned the Black dolls. The results were so stark that they influenced the deliberations of the 1954 *Brown v. Board of Education* case, which led to the desegregation of American schools.[16] And, unfortunately, this isn't just ancient history: A more recent 2005 documentary film called *A Girl Like Me* recorded similar experiments with similar results.[17]

Internalized racism has destructive consequences for both individuals and communities. For individuals, internalized racism is associated with anxiety, depression, shame, low self-esteem, and other poor health outcomes.[18] And did you know that internalized racism can even pit people of color against each other? One well-known example is the **crabs-in-a-bucket effect.** If you put a bunch of crabs in a bucket, they will do their best to escape. One crab in a bucket can escape without a problem. But a group of crabs in a bucket will drag down any individual crab that tries to escape—irrationally ensuring the demise of the whole group! I believe this may be one reason that my most vicious bully growing up was not White but Black. And my Oreo label is not unique, unfortunately. There are a number of other racial slurs that derive from food products. You can check them out at the online Racial Slur Database (don't you love the internet?).[19] Painfully similar epithets for people being "ethnic" on the outside but White on the inside are apples (Indigenous peoples), bananas (Asians), and coconuts (Latinos and South Asians), to name a few.

Colorism is another form of internalized racism that assigns higher value to lighter skin tones, with grievous consequences.[20] It is already true that "dark-skinned blacks have lower levels of education, income, and job status. They are less likely to own homes or to marry; and dark-skinned blacks' prison sentences are longer."[21] However, internalized racism is notorious for prompting even people of color to discriminate against their own darker-skinned counterparts.[22]

Sadly, internalized racism causes many to betray their own. Some pursue **assimilation,** which means downplaying your ethnic distinctiveness in order to better fit in with the dominant group. Others go further through **defensive othering,** which means distancing yourself from your own racial group. Hate or shame for one's own community is, in many ways, the final frontier of racism. Tragically, in this way, racism causes many people of color to say: *If you can't beat 'em, join 'em.*

YES, TRAUMA ALSO COMES IN WHITE

When it comes to trauma, we are right to think about victims first. Yet trauma harms victimizers too. Why is that? Because God created humans to experience loving community as equals. He did *not* create people to marginalize and oppress one another. Whenever we do that, we go against God's design—and there is always some kind of "price" to pay.

---

*When God's design for equality is broken,
there is a price that the victimizer
must pay.*

Let's consider an example from the book of Exodus. For hundreds of years, the Israelites have been enslaved in Egypt, suffering deep trauma as a minority group. When God sends Moses to deliver them, the story focuses on Moses's negotiations with Pharaoh. Of course, the text highlights the trauma that the *victim,* Israel, suffers. Yet it also clearly depicts how oppressing others traumatizes the *victimizer,* Pharaoh, too. We can see it in the progressive hardening of Pharaoh's heart. We see it in Pharaoh's unrelenting pride, denial, and delusion. We see it as Pharaoh desperately continues to embrace a false narrative of superiority, one that he simply cannot bear to give up. Pharaoh may be in power—but he is also in trouble. He is lost, and ultimately he is unable to cope with reality. In the end, the trauma that Pharaoh has inflicted boomerangs right back to him—and leads to the downfall of the entire nation!

Today, psychologists call this **perpetrator trauma** or **Perpetration-Induced Traumatic Stress (PITS),** a form of post-traumatic stress syndrome (PTSD) that emerges after a person traumatizes someone else. If we understand White Americans to be another traumatized group, we might more sympathetically recognize in them certain symptoms of trauma. For example, we might better understand certain reactions that Whites often have when confronted with racial inequity: shock, denial, avoidance, delusion, guilt, shame, and more. These are trauma responses. The truth is that the trauma of racism "has resulted in large numbers of Americans who are white, racist, and proud to be both; an even larger number who are white, racist, and in reflexive denial about it; and another large number who are white, progressive, and ashamed of their whiteness. All of these are forms of immaturity; all can be trauma responses; and all harm African Americans *and* white Americans."[23]

Color-courageous disciples recognize that we *all* need healing from the trauma that racism has caused—whether we realize it or not. We are all equal at the foot of the cross, and we all need God's healing touch.

SHEDDING LIGHT ON SHAME

One of the most harmful consequences of trauma is shame. Brené Brown's well-known definition of **shame** has resonated with millions of people: "the intensely painful feeling or experience of believing that we are flawed and therefore unworthy of love and belonging—something we've experienced, done, or failed to do makes us unworthy of connection."[24] Ever since Eden, we humans have been seeking to avoid shame at all costs.

Since God's heart is to *foster* shalom, you can be sure that the Enemy's plan is to *unravel* shalom. And shame is one of his most effective strategies. Just as racism has caused trauma for both people of color and for Whites, so too has our trauma produced shame in us all. To experience shalom, color-courageous disciples must acknowledge not only racial trauma but also the racial shame that trauma causes.

To experience shalom, color-courageous disciples must acknowledge not only racial trauma but also the racial shame that trauma causes.

What does shame look like for people of color? As a woman of color, throughout my life, I have been tempted to believe the powerful false narrative that I am worth less—or, in other words, *worthless.* My trauma provoked the painful thought: *Perhaps there really is something wrong with me.* My pursuit of perfection was my fig leaf of choice to cover the shame of who I was.

But shame impacts the racially privileged too. Racial shame plays out in White communities, for example, in a number of ways. One way is through shame about the past. As White individuals begin to recognize how they or their predecessors have consciously or unconsciously perpetuated racial inequity, shame rears its ugly head. An important distinction: It is *healthy* to feel grief over past mistakes; it is *unhealthy* to feel shame (see 2 Corinthians 7:10).

Another form of shame that impacts White disciples who seek to become color-courageous is the fear of making mistakes. But ironically, this fear of making mistakes can make racial reconciliation even harder! In *White Fragility,* Robin DiAngelo talks about the dynamic of the good/bad binary that so often stymies antiracism efforts—the idea that if someone points out racism in me, then I must be "bad" rather than "good." Not only is this ridiculously simplistic, but it also misses the point that growth over time involves a bumpy process of making mistakes, falling, and getting back up again. Andrew Horning, the author of *Grappling: White Men's Journey from Fragile to Agile,* unpacks this:

> We have to realize "I can be a good person *and* have racist patterns"... learned behavior that can be unlearned.... The feeling of discomfort or possibly shame is only a temporary state, and if we can sustain ourselves through it, we can come out the other side confident and free.[25]

Many people avoid getting started with antiracist work because they are afraid of feeling shame. They are afraid that they will somehow make a mistake along the way—and then be called racist! Ironic, right? This is a type of shame that must be dealt with head-on. No one is perfect, and we will all make mistakes as we learn and grow. Regardless of race, color-courageous disciples of all backgrounds will be effective to the extent that they identify and heal their shame, exchanging it for something better.

HEALING OUR STORIES, HEALING OUR SOULS

To deal with trauma and shame, we must experience **rediscipleship** through the exchange of false stories for true ones. As we have discussed previously, racism is not only a false idea; it is an entirely false story. That is why we can't only address our practices. We must also address the story itself, the story that is making us sick. In this way, color-courageous discipleship becomes an exercise of reimagination.

We must address the story itself, the story that is making us sick.

Over the centuries, the narrative of racial difference has led to experiences of racial trauma for us all. To find healing, we must take ownership of our own stories together with God—lest we remain "trapped as characters in stories someone else is telling."[26] In the process, we can also "own our stories of falling down, screwing up, and facing hurt so we can integrate those stories into our lives and write daring new endings."[27]

Why is it so hard to own our own stories of falling down, screwing up, and facing hurt? Because doing so requires courage. I love how our word *courage* derives from *cor,* the Latin word for heart. In fact, "In one of its earliest forms, the word *courage* meant 'To speak one's mind by telling all one's heart.'"[28] What this means is that color-courageous discipleship is not only about performing valiant deeds. It is also about *being vulnerable.* It is about choosing to acknowledge, own, and share the stories of our own hearts, stories that we might otherwise be ashamed of. We do this both for the sake of our own healing and so that we might extend that healing to the world.

Let's now consider two of the fundamental stories that we must recover to find healing.

Story #1: We are created in the image of God. All my life, I've heard that I am "made in the image of God." But . . . so what? It's kind of like hearing someone say, "You have the same nose as your dad!" It's cute to recognize, but it doesn't make any real difference to my life. But now, I'm beginning to get it. Being created in the **image of God** means that we reflect the royalty of God, that we are called to be royal characters in God's story.

The story of racial difference denies that we are all equally created in the image of God, pointing to "race" as an important way to measure our value. But the truth is that our value is not a matter of pedigree, race, or achievement. Our royal identity is grounded in the image of God. Knowing at my core that I'm royalty? That you are royalty? That people of every ethnicity, culture, and background were created to reflect God's royal image *in unique ways* and that no one can take that away from us? Yes, that makes a difference!

Story #2: We are deeply loved by God. God's love is the deep narrative that lies at the center of the cosmos and is the narrative beneath all narratives. God's love surrounds us like an ocean, working out his good purposes in us and through all that happens. Listen to what the Bible says about this: "We know that in all things God works for the good of those who love him, who have been called according to his purpose" (Romans 8:28). In fact, nothing in the entire universe can separate us from God's love (Romans 8:39). We will become increasingly free to the extent that we live into this truth. A Christian writer by the name of Henri Nouwen put it beautifully. He wrote that "becoming the Beloved is the great spiritual journey we have to make."[29] God is still speaking over us the same words that he spoke over Christ: *You are my beloved, in you I am well-pleased* (Matthew 3:17). We must learn to attune our hearts to that voice:

> It is certainly not easy to hear that voice in a world filled with voices that shout: "You are no good, you are ugly, you are worthless, you are despicable, you are nobody—unless you can demonstrate the opposite." . . . Self-rejection is the greatest enemy of the spiritual life because it contradicts the sacred voice that calls us the "Beloved." Being the Beloved expresses the core truth of our existence.[30]

And then, when we embrace our identity as God's beloved, we can also more easily embrace **post-traumatic growth**—the positive transformation that can be experienced *as a result* of the struggle with a traumatic event.[31] Isn't that amazing? God can actually bring about growth from some of the most challenging experiences of our lives. Think about it: From one vantage point, the entire Bible is a story of post-traumatic growth! It's the story of how God continues to grow his good purposes in the world even *after* the great tragedy of the Fall. And, of course, we now follow a Savior whose death—the most traumatic event in history—has made possible the salvation of the entire world.

We cannot force post-traumatic growth to happen, but we can intentionally foster growth as we reframe our stories in light of God's love.

We cannot *force* post-traumatic growth to happen, but we can intentionally *foster* growth as we reframe our stories in light of God's love. The result can be the rediscovery of beauty from the ashes. That does not mean pretending that everything is okay. What it *does* mean is that as we tell our stories, "we [can be] transformed from victims of uncontrollable events into well-informed authors, and our life stories [can] become meaningful works of art."[32]

In light of God's love, I know for certain that no events of my story will prove to be pointless. Instead, my story—*every single part*—is becoming a meaningful work of art in God's hands. No chapter of my story has ever been lived outside of the reach of God's love. But God is able to transform the pain that I have endured into a means of extending God's love to others. What wonderful news!

Trauma is never good, but trauma can be repurposed into a redemptive force.

Trauma is never good, but trauma can be repurposed into a redemptive force. This truth echoes the famous words of Joseph, who was so deeply traumatized by his own brothers: "You intended to harm me, but God intended it for good to accomplish what is now being done, the saving of many lives" (Genesis 50:20). Even through our trauma, our foundational truth is that we are caught up in the story of God's love.

THE FREEDOM OF FORGIVENESS

The cross bears witness to the truth that forgiveness is what ultimately brings lasting healing and freedom. Returning to our story of Jesus and the paralytic: What the paralytic wanted was to walk again. Instead, Jesus proclaimed, "Your sins are forgiven!" Jesus understands that true healing entails *forgiveness.* "Forgive us our sins, for we also forgive everyone who sins against us" (Luke 11:4)—these are perhaps the most liberating words we can pray.

"Forgive us our sins": When we are forgiven by God, we are liberated from sin, which is our true disease. Jesus died for not only the sin of the world *out there* but also the sin *in here,* the sin that is present and active in every human heart and leads only to death (Romans 6:23). Undeserved forgiveness is the beating heart of our faith (Romans 5:8).

An important note: Color-courageous disciples must also remain alert to the *subtler sins* that are likely to infect our own hearts. No, we may no longer engage in obvious racial prejudice . . . but we can all too easily fall into the less obvious (though equally poisonous) sins of self-righteousness and pride, thinking that we are better than others who don't "get it" yet. "Forgive us our sins" applies to us all—on every point of the color-courageous discipleship journey.

"For we also forgive everyone who sins against us": Forgiveness places us firmly on the path to the ultimate goal: restored relation-

ships in a beloved community. But we can only enjoy restored relationships as we acknowledge that we are all equal at the foot of the cross; we are all sinners in need of God's forgiveness. Beloved community is the end goal, and our courageous choice to forgive is what makes beloved community possible. In the words of King: "We can never say, 'I will forgive you, but I won't have anything further to do with you.' Forgiveness means reconciliation, a coming together again."[33] As South African leader Desmond Tutu put it, there can be "no future without forgiveness."[34]

DESMOND TUTU: NO FUTURE WITHOUT FORGIVENESS

Desmond Tutu*
PHOTO: © JOHN
MATHEW SMITH,
2001

Desmond Tutu (1931–2021) was a South African Anglican bishop, theologian, and Christian civil rights leader. He was renowned for his ministry as an anti-apartheid activist. Apartheid was a legal system of racial segregation and discrimination that existed in South Africa all the way through the early 1990s. When apartheid fell, many predicted that the country would descend into chaos. South Africans of color finally had their opportunity for revenge! But to everyone's surprise, that is *not* what happened—largely thanks to the wise leadership of Desmond Tutu. Through his work with South Africa's Truth and Reconciliation Commission, victimizers were inspired to confess, apologize, and make amends, while victims were inspired to extend forgiveness. Why? So that the community could move forward together in healing, love, and freedom. As Tutu insisted, there simply can be "no future without forgiveness."[35]

* https://commons.wikimedia.org/wiki/File:Desmond_Tutu_1997.jpg

FLOURISHING AS WOUNDED HEALERS

Have you ever read George Orwell's classic book *Animal Farm*? It is a brilliant cautionary fable. A summary: A barnful of animals becomes fed up with the oppressive regime of the farmers. Led by the pigs, the animals successfully overthrow the farmers. In time, however, the pigs gradually adopt the same values and practices of the farmers—until they themselves form a new ruling oppressive class that is indistinguishable from the old one. The pigs even wear the farmers' clothes and sleep in the farmers' beds!

While seeking to defeat evil, we must not in the process become ensnared by evil.

What happened was this: In fighting evil, they became evil themselves. This is precisely the pattern that color-courageous disciples must resist, as Martin Luther King, Jr., taught his followers in *Strength to Love:* "Forced to live with these shameful conditions, we are tempted to become bitter and to retaliate with a corresponding hate. But if this happens, the new order we seek will be little more than a duplicate of the old order. We must in strength and humility meet hate with love."[36]

While seeking to defeat evil, we must not in the process become ensnared by evil. It is the very nature of evil to do this. This is why inner healing is so vital for color-courageous discipleship: so that we might not be overcome by evil, but overcome evil with good (Romans 12:21). To heal the world, we begin with humility, restoration, repentance, and forgiveness. In other words, we begin healing the world as we experience healing ourselves.

Perhaps one reason that Jesus continued to visibly bear the scars of the trauma he suffered—even after the resurrection—is to demonstrate that as his followers, we, too, can become wounded healers.

"Do not be overcome by evil, but overcome evil with good."

As we continue to experience the healing of God, we can extend that healing to others and build communities that seek to heal the world. As we go deeper into God's love and courageously extend that same love to others, we can become co-builders of that which God has envisioned for us: a rich and colorful beloved community.

THINK ABOUT IT

1. "Only through an inner spiritual transformation do we gain the strength to fight vigorously the evils of the world in a humble and loving spirit." How would you explain this quote by Martin Luther King, Jr., to someone else?

2. Why is it important to understand the trauma that people of color have experienced, past and present? How does understanding the trauma of people of all backgrounds help us to love well?

3. Do you think that you or your friends may have experienced racial trauma? What would it look like to pursue healing?

4. Why is it important to replace the false stories in our heads and hearts with true stories? What difference does it make? In what ways would you like to do this?

5. Desmond Tutu taught that there is "no future without forgiveness." In your own words, what does that mean?

DISCIPLESHIP AS BELOVED COMMUNITY

Experience Christ-Shaped Solidarity

> The end is reconciliation; the end is redemption; the end
> is the creation of the beloved community.
> —MARTIN LUTHER KING, JR., "FACING THE CHALLENGE OF A NEW AGE"

Any discipleship journey must ultimately find its destination in love. For Jesus, love was the point. As Jesus taught us, love of God and love of neighbor are the greatest commandments. These are a pair that can never be separated (Matthew 22:36–40). Everything else in the Christian life is a footnote to love.

As we have learned, a Christian approach to antiracism entails both dismantling something *and* building something. So, we seek to dismantle racism and to build . . . what? As Martin Luther King, Jr., increasingly emphasized toward the end of his life, above all else, our aim as color-courageous disciples of Christ must be to build beloved community:

> I do not think of political power as an end. Neither do I think of economic power as an end. They are ingredients in the objective that we seek in life. And I think that end of that objective is a truly brotherly society, the creation of the beloved community.[1]

I have often wondered: What distinguishes a Christian approach to antiracism from any other approach? One distinguishing mark of Christian antiracism is our destination: *a beloved community characterized by Christlike love.* Unfortunately, today *love* means different things to different people. That is why, on this leg of the journey, we will recenter ourselves on how *God* envisions love.

Now, for me, the only way to talk about love is just like the Scriptures do—with poetry. Did you know that the Bible actually begins with a poem? Scholars understand that the creation account in Genesis 1 actually has the cadence of a beautifully structured poem. So, just as the Bible begins with a poem, we will also begin with a poetic reimagining of humanity's creation by love and for love—a poem in three acts.

GOD'S POETRY

Did you know that approximately 30 percent of the Bible is poetry? Perhaps that is because poetry is the language of love, and the Bible is God's love letter to the world! There are six books of the Bible that are entirely poetry—Job, Psalms, Proverbs, Ecclesiastes, Song of Songs, and Lamentations. Poetry is a wonderful tool for saying things that are hard to say in any other way. The poetic books of the Bible portray both dark feelings (like grief and despair) as well as bright ones (like passion and joy). Sometimes, it's nearly impossible to put our emotions and experiences into words; only a poem or song will do.

Act I: Created by Love

Before the beginning, there was Love—glorious, rejoicing, beautiful Love.
A tripersonal community, an everlasting embrace, a Beloved Community.
Listen closely, and you can hear its cadence . . .
the gentle beating heart at the center of the universe.
Unity-in-diversity. Unity, not uniformity.
Three partners
delighting in difference, savoring the dance.
Love lacked nothing, required nothing.
Love was satisfied.
Yet this love could not be contained!
So Love overflowed in a burst of fire and light.
Love took a three-dimensional canvas and painted:
day and night, sky and sea, flora and fauna, and then the crown—
Man and Woman
delighting in difference, savoring the dance.
And Love flared into song
over its children:
"Welcome to Beloved Community!
In you, I am well pleased!
You are blessed
'to love and to multiply Beloved Community
throughout the earth!"
And Love rejoiced in the goodness and wonder of
its manifold masterpiece.

Our God is triune love—Father, Son, and Holy Spirit, a beloved community existing in an eternal trinitarian embrace. This is what the Bible teaches: "God is love. Whoever lives in love lives in God, and God in them" (1 John 4:16). In this, we discover an astonishing truth: *We were created by and for beloved community.* Of course, the kingdom of God will only be fully realized when Jesus returns. Yet we live in the era of the "already but not yet," which means that although the kingdom of God is *present* in the world, it is not yet *pervasive*. Still, color–courageous disciples are called to bear witness to God's reign even now.

A point of clarification: Is the "kingdom of God" the same thing as "beloved community"? For me, they do overlap, but they are slightly different. Beloved community is a dimension of the larger kingdom of God. The **kingdom of God** is the overarching term for the rule of Jesus Christ that includes every dimension of creation. **Beloved community,** on the other hand, narrows our focus to how a diverse community of people interacts with one another in God's kingdom.

Our focus has been on how racism impedes beloved community. But to truly pull up racism from the roots, we must understand the shape of the sin that lies at those roots. Is that sin hatred? Disgust? Envy? Apathy? Ibram X. Kendi, author of *How to Be an Antiracist,* has wrestled for years to identify the roots of racism. Although he does not write from a Christian perspective, his conclusion on this question does sound similar to what the Bible says: "My research kept pointing me to the same answer: The source of racist ideas [is] not ignorance and hate, but self-interest."[2] Compare that with the Bible in James 3:16: "For where jealousy and self-interest exist, there will be disorder and every evil thing" (BLB).

This is a powerful insight: *The opposite of beloved community is self-interest.* Now by "self-interest" I am not talking about caring for oneself in normal and natural ways. The word translated as "self-interest" in James 3:16 is *eritheia,* the pursuit of one's own interests with little to no regard for the interests of others. In other words, sin turns us inward. Our sin nature inclines us to look out for ourselves, even when it disadvantages others. In beloved community, on the other hand, we lovingly look out for others even when it disadvantages ourselves. Beloved community turns outward in a posture of generosity and embrace.

But let's think about this some more: *Why* are we inclined inward? *Because we are afraid.* We live in a fallen world. We are vulnerable to scarcity, suffering, sickness, and death—so it makes perfect sense that we would be afraid in this world. Yet the greatest tragedy of fear is that it frustrates our ability to love, just like the Bible says: "The one who fears is not made perfect in love" (1 John 4:18). Fear destroys the very possibility of beloved community. How can I share with you, honor you, pay attention to you, sacrifice for you if I fear that these same things won't be done for me?

I believe that the author George Yancey has correctly named the "fear factor" as the final frontier of racial reconciliation.[3] For example, in conversations about race, White people may fear being misunderstood or labeled a racist, or shunned for committing a racial faux pas. They may also fear the consequences of making waves with their White friends. People of color may fear being dismissed, discounted, or labeled a troublemaker. And, of course, they may fear that all their efforts will not yield any results in the end. And here's the thing: *These are all real possibilities.* Not only do we live in a broken world, but the sin that resides deep within every human heart means that we will hurt each other on the journey toward beloved community. Our pattern, in Yancey's words, is to perpetuate a vicious "cycle of fear."[4] What, then, can break the cycle of fear? *Only love.* Which is why, in Christ, God took definitive action to cast out our fears with love—and make us courageous (1 John 4:18, ESV).

Act II: Redeemed by Love

But one day
we accepted the Lie:
"God is not Love, and you are not the Beloved."
We turned away from God to self.

We turned away from neighbor to self.
And then self asked: "Am I my brother's keeper?"
We barely noticed our exchange of faith for fear:
fear of God, fear of death, and fear of one another.
So much fear.
Self-interest—born.
Beloved Community—broken.
But Love
launched a plan!
A plan to redeem and restore
Beloved Community
rebuilt on faith and sacrificial love.
And Love spread its arms as wide as the cross
casting out fear
forever
filling us with courage
and empowering us to rebuild Beloved Community
together.

The love that grounds God's beloved community is love of a particular kind. The love of beloved community is **agape love,** the self-giving, sacrificial, supernatural love of God that casts out all fear (1 John 4:18). While our broken world pressures us to succumb to the slavery of self-interest, it is agape love that frees us to be like Christ—to look not to our own interests but "to the interests of the others" (Philippians 2:4).

The ultimate goal of color-courageous discipleship, like all discipleship, is the expression of agape love. Consider this: Jesus taught plenty of former commands in new ways, but only once did he claim to establish a "new command." And that new command was about agape love: "A new command I give you: Love one another. As I have loved you, so you must love one another" (John 13:34). But what, exactly, made this love command "new"? After all, Jesus spoke about love before, right?

THE DIVERSITY OF LOVE

Did you know that in the Bible there are at least four different words that we can translate into English as "love"? You can read more about them in *The Four Loves* by C. S. Lewis!

The Four Types of Love in the Bible

EROS
romantic love, passion between lovers

STORGE
familial love, between family members

PHILIA
brotherly love, affection between friends

AGAPE
self-sacrificial love, God's love

Of course he did. So, to be clear, what made this command new was that Jesus was establishing *himself* as the standard—the very definition—of love! Jesus transformed love from an abstract idea to a concrete picture by pointing to his own life. Jesus's new command was to love not in some abstract way but just like he loves. Jesus says: *My new command is this. Don't just love in some vague, generic way. Love in precisely the same way that I have loved you.*

And how did Jesus love us? By dying an excruciating death on the cross. He loved us by forgiving those who had hurt him. He loved us by suffering, sacrificing, and shedding his own blood. That just doesn't sound like a recipe for living your best life! Yet the kingdom of Christ is an upside-down kingdom. Jesus loved us like this "for the joy set before him" (Hebrews 12:2). Through his death, he paved the way to both eternal life *and* beloved community.

As Jesus-followers, we are not called to comfortable discipleship. We are called to cruciform discipleship. **Cruciform** discipleship is discipleship in the shape of the cross. As Christ-followers, we are called to love like Jesus with agape love, to suffer and sacrifice for the joy set before us.

We are not called to comfortable discipleship.
We are called to cruciform discipleship.

God has promised to meet our every need according to the riches of his glory in Christ Jesus (Philippians 4:19). This empowers us to practice agape love. We need not exhaust ourselves in self-interest; we can look to the interests of others. Still, sometimes it certainly doesn't *feel* like God is supplying our every need! That's why we can only love like Jesus by faith. If Christ did not rise from the dead, then our faith is futile (1 Corinthians 15:17). If Christ did not rise, then it makes sense to look out for number one. But Christ *did* rise. There is life beyond this life. As we set our minds "on things above, not on earthly things," we will be free to love like Christ loved (Colossians 3:2). Color-courageous disciples build beloved community *by faith*.

The enemy of our souls seeks to stymie the creation of beloved community by prompting us to answer no to the same question that Cain asked: "Am I my brother's keeper?" But our

God whispers a different response: *Yes, a thousand times yes! It is by becoming your brother's keeper that you build beloved community and experience fullness of life.*

One way to practice agape love in our journey toward beloved community is to create safe, courageous spaces where we can talk openly and honestly about our fears.[5] These spaces must be characterized by grace and be where people can connect without fear of judgment or reprisal. The ultimate goal? To lay the foundations for a beloved community, a community that by definition casts out fear with love.

Self-interest, rooted in fear, is normal and natural. But disciples are called to that which is supernatural. Color-courageous disciples, in a posture of agape love, look not only to their "own interests" but also "to the interests of the others" (Philippians 2:4).

As God's love pours into us by the power of his Spirit, and overflows to others, we will find that beloved community begins to take shape. This is a beautiful parallel to Pentecost, which launches us into Act III:

Act III: Called to Become Beloved Community

Behold: Pentecost!
Behold beloved community recreated
in fire and light.
Behold God's chosen ones, holy and beloved
from every tribe, tongue, people, and nation
now being transformed from glory to glory,
delighting in difference, savoring the dance.
Behold the Body of Christ reincarnate,
empowered by the Spirit,
and entrusted with a Great and Colorful Commission:
You are blessed to love in living color!
You are blessed to go and build beloved community.

PENTECOST

Happy birthday to the church! The church was born on a day we call Pentecost. Pentecost was originally a Jewish holiday on which people traditionally celebrated the harvest as well as God's giving of the law (the Ten Commandments) to Israel. After his death and resurrection, Jesus told the disciples to wait and pray for the power they needed to fulfill his mission to make disciples of all nations. On the day of Pentecost, God poured out his Holy Spirit on the disciples as tongues of fire! This event marked the birth of the church, and it clearly signaled that God's intention was for the church to embrace people from every tribe, tongue, people, and nation.

BUILDING BELOVED COMMUNITY

We are privileged to live now in the third act—the age of Pentecost. At Pentecost, God filled the disciples with his Spirit. This Spirit gives us the power to actually *become* beloved community. But what does that look like?

We can glean some wisdom on this from Paul's first letter to the Corinthians. The Corinthian congregation was gifted and vibrant, but it was also deeply divided. Throughout 1 Corinthians, Paul addressed divisions of all kinds. He called out division and disorder relating to apostolic authority, gender, class, sexual holiness, worship preferences, and ethnicity. His letter was designed to address their multiple divisions and move them toward agape love. To do that, he urged them to behold the beautiful poetic metaphor of the body of Christ—which is a great thing for us to do too!

In this metaphor, the Holy Spirit is key: Disciples are only forged into the body of Christ *by the power of the Holy Spirit.* In

Paul's words, "For we were all baptized by one Spirit so as to form one body—whether Jews or Gentles, slave or free—and we were all given the one Spirit to drink" (1 Corinthians 12:13).

Also, before diving in, let's remember that as color-courageous disciples, we do not build beloved community *in our own power.* Still, the language of "building" is profoundly biblical. The Bible teaches that when the body of Christ is healthy, it *"builds itself up in love,* as each part does its work" (Ephesians 4:16). By the power of the Holy Spirit, we are all called to build beloved community— each one of us doing our part, whatever our age or stage in life might be.

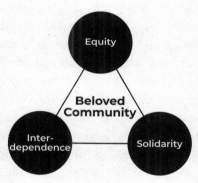

Through the poetry of 1 Corinthians 12, we discover three timeless characteristics of the body of Christ: **solidarity, inter-dependence,** and **equity.** These words might be new to you, but don't worry, we're about to explore each one. As we do, we will discover that color-courageous disciples can build beloved community by engaging in these three paradigm shifts:

1. **From separation to solidarity:** "We are one body"
2. **From independence to interdependence:** "We need each other"
3. **From equality to equity:** "We love best when we love some differently"

I highly recommend that you take a look at 1 Corinthians 12 as you read along and reflect on these three characteristics of beloved community.

1. From Separation to Solidarity: "We Are One Body"

A body, by definition, is one. So, in 1 Corinthians 12, Paul painted a picture of a dual truth: The church is made up of diverse parts *and* the church operates as one body. The fact is this: Whether we realize it or not, as disciples of Jesus, we are *already* one body. It's just a simple statement of fact. To the extent that we neglect reality and behave like completely separate members, our body will malfunction. On the other hand, to the extent that we acknowledge and deepen our fundamental connectedness, we will experience greater health and life.

It is obviously ludicrous for one part of the body to remain indifferent to the well-being of the other parts. *A hurting body part always eventually impacts the whole.* It just makes sense that each member of the body "should have equal concern for each other" (12:25). And what, exactly, does equal concern look like? Paul told us: "If one part suffers, every part suffers with it; if one part is honored, every part rejoices with it" (12:26).

This is what Martin Luther King, Jr., meant when he said that "injustice anywhere is a threat to justice everywhere."[6]

> To the degree that I harm my brother, no matter what he is doing to me, to that extent I am harming myself. . . . Why is this? Because all men are brothers. If you harm me, you harm yourself. Love, *agape,* is the only cement that can hold this broken community together.[7]

This is the part of the journey where **solidarity** comes in. *Solidarity means intentionally living into the reality that we are already* *deeply connected, for the good of the whole.* Although Paul was talking in 1 Corinthians 12 about the body of Christ, solidarity is vital for the health of any diverse community. Caring for one another just makes sense.

Members of beloved community learn to both acknowledge and own the suffering of other members.

As time passes, we continue to discover new dimensions of our fundamental connectedness. In her brilliant book *The Sum of Us: What Racism Costs Everyone and How We Can Prosper Together,* Heather McGhee presents evidence for how racism hurts everyone—not just people of color—in tangible ways.[8] The secular world inclines toward a **zero-sum paradigm:** "If I gain, you lose. If you gain, I lose." But in reality, racial zero-sum thinking leads to a lower quality of life for all racial groups. McGhee illustrates how this currently happens in nearly every sector, including education, housing, labor, public recreation, and the environment. Instead, she encourages us to pursue *solidarity,* the "gains that come when people come together across race, to accomplish what we simply can't do on our own."[9] Another example is the book *Dying of Whiteness,* in which Jonathan Metzl demonstrates the surprising ways in which racism toward people of color has backfired to harm White communities in healthcare and education too.[10]

To summarize: Just as a body operates as a whole and naturally cares for itself, so a beloved community operates as a whole and naturally cares for itself. Members of beloved community learn to both acknowledge—*and own*—the suffering of other members.

2. From Independence to Interdependence: "We Need Each Other"

We Americans love our independence! We resist the idea that we "need" anybody else to thrive. However, this does not reflect a biblical worldview, as 1 Corinthians 12 demonstrates. Robin DiAngelo, too, points out what extreme independence costs us when it comes to race:

> The most profound message of racial segregation may be that the absence of people of color from our lives is no real loss. Not one person who loved me, guided me, or taught me ever conveyed that segregation deprived me of anything of value. I could live my entire life without a friend or loved one of color and not see that as a diminishment of my life.[11]

Independence has its place, but members of the body of Christ have a higher calling to interdependence.

Here's the truth: The conviction that we lose nothing as we live segregated lives is a diabolical lie that diminishes our lives. As Paul said, "The eye *cannot* say to the hand, 'I don't need you!' And the head *cannot* say to the feet, 'I don't need you!'" (1 Corinthians 12:21). Independence has its place, but members of the body of Christ have a higher calling to interdependence. It is a great mystery that "those parts of the body that seem to be weaker are indispensable" (12:22):

> There are different kinds of gifts, but the same Spirit distributes them. There are different kinds of service, but the same Lord. There are different kinds of working, but in all of them and in

everyone it is the same God at work. *Now to each one the mani-festation of the Spirit is given for the common good.* (12:4–7)

The word translated as "manifestation" in verse 7 is literally *revelation.* I love that. The word *revelation* emphasizes an important truth: It is impossible to know in advance precisely how the gifts of each member of the body will benefit the whole. This is something that only God reveals along the way. What we do know is that the strong members of the body are blessed by those who are "weaker," often in unexpected ways. In God's economy, it is the poor who are richly blessed—which para-doxically means that the "poor" have much to share with the larger body (Luke 6:20). Jesus even taught that in caring for "the least of these," we have the opportunity to encounter him (Matthew 25:31–46).

Remember our definition of *ethnicity:* a God-ordained cul-tural identity that God delights in as a means for bringing glory to himself and enrichment to his kingdom. This is meant to be experienced in the diverse, interdependent body of Christ. How can we do more to delight in ethnic diversity as a means of bringing greater enrichment to the whole body? Color-courageous disciples seek to dismantle racism so that we can all experience the riches of a colorful community.

Of course, racial and ethnic categories are just one way of thinking about "stronger" and "weaker" members of the body of Christ. In his writings, Henri Nouwen reflected upon the riches he gained by moving from Yale to a caring community for dis-abled people called L'Arche. While Yale is one of the most pres-tigious institutions in the world, L'Arche represents a community of people who tend to be devalued and even despised by society. In the eyes of the world, moving there was a completely irratio-nal decision! Nevertheless, Nouwen came to understand the move to be *his gain:*

L'Arche exists not to help the mentally handicapped get "normal," but to help them share their spiritual gifts with the world. The poor of spirit are given to us for *our* conversion. In their poverty, the mentally handicapped reveal God to us and hold us close to the Gospel.[12]

It was while he was at L'Arche that Nouwen learned many of his greatest spiritual lessons. God calls us, both as individuals and communities, to live in solidarity with everyone, but especially with "the least of these," just as Jesus prioritized the least of these in his relationships. When we do, we will be blessed in unexpected ways.

Let's be sure, though, to remember that the opposite is also true. Just as the strong need the weak, so too do the weak need the strong. We all need each other. At times, people of color have become very tired of the status quo—justifiably—and have embraced racial separation too! Fed up with the body as a whole, some people might prefer to stop identifying with the body entirely. Yet Paul had words for this tendency too:

Now if the foot should say, "Because I am not a hand, I do not belong to the body," *it would not for that reason stop being part of the body.* And if the ear should say, "Because I am not an eye, I do not belong to the body," it would not for that reason stop being part of the body. (1 Corinthians 12:15–16)

Regardless of our placement in the body—whether we consider ourselves weaker or stronger, more advantaged or less—we still mysteriously *need* the rich and surprising gifts that God grants to us only in and through one another.

3. From Equality to Equity: "We Love Best When We Love Some Differently"

A common objection to antiracism is that it results in what some call **reverse racism.** They claim, for example, that antiracism initiatives simply exchange an unfair preference for Whites with an unfair preference for Blacks. This is an important concern, so let's address it.

It is true that color-courageous disciples must be careful not to exchange one type of injustice for another type of injustice. At the same time, biblical equity does not preclude the need for *customized treatment* in all cases. We've already seen that equality emphasizes *sameness* while equity emphasizes *fairness.* To be certain, both have their place. At first glance, sameness seems appropriate—everyone should receive the same treatment, right? Actually, though, this logic works best in situations where everyone enjoys a similar starting point. Check out this image of three guys trying to watch a baseball game over a fence. Giving the same footstool to everybody doesn't make much sense . . . at least not if the goal is for everyone to actually see the game![13]

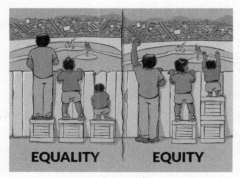

Interaction Institute for Social Change
Artist: Angus Maguire

In the baseball game example, we see that *equal* footstools actually result in vastly *unequal* outcomes. What would be more helpful here is *equity*—a fair *opportunity* for everyone to watch the game. In our illustration, this would require a customized stool for each person.

Let's be clear: I am not talking about forcing everyone toward the same outcomes regardless of their efforts. The goal, rather, is fairness. We want everyone to have a fair *opportunity* to be rewarded for their efforts. So let's put it all together. **Equality** is about *sameness,* treating everyone the same no matter what. **Equity** is about *fairness,* giving everyone the opportunity for a fair shot in an unfair world.

Our baseball game illustration is not perfect, of course, and many have suggested other metaphors that you might prefer. This is just one way to depict how, at times, *equal concern is best expressed through customized treatment.* But don't take my word for it. We can discover this very idea in 1 Corinthians 12. As you read these verses, notice the repetition of the word *special:*

> The parts that we think are less honorable we treat with *special* honor. And the parts that are unpresentable are treated with *special* modesty, while our presentable parts need no *special* treatment. But God has put the body together, giving *greater honor* to the parts that lacked it, so that there should be no division in the body, but that its parts should have *equal concern* for each other. (1 Corinthians 12:23–25)

The concept of special treatment occurs here three times, in addition to the concept of giving greater honor to some—precisely in order to express "equal concern for each other" (verse 25). In Western cultures, many have a negative knee-jerk reaction when a person or group receives special treatment. Yet God's economy is countercultural. The Scriptures teach that a healthy, fair, and caring community—that is, a beloved community—actually requires "special treatment" and "greater honor" for some members, at least some of the time (12:24).

Equality is about sameness, *treating everyone the same no matter what. Equity is about* fairness, *giving everyone the opportunity for a fair shot in an unfair world.*

Some might ask, "When does it end? Must we now give people of color special treatment indefinitely? Isn't this just a form of reverse racism?" These are good questions. We don't want to simply switch the categories of who's permanently on top and who's permanently at the bottom. We have already explored how all human beings possess a sin nature, both individually and corporately, so there is always the possibility for a former victim to become a victimizer.

That is why we must keep our goal clearly before us. The goal is not to replace one unjust system with another unjust system. The goal is biblical equity. When everyone enjoys a fair opportunity, then, theoretically, special treatment will no longer be needed. However, assuming that this goal *could* be reached in a broken world, it would sadly take a very long time to get there—just as it has taken us a very long time to get to where we find ourselves now.

In one of his final speeches, Martin Luther King, Jr., directly addressed the argument that the Black community should not receive any special treatment to better their condition. He countered with this:

> Now there is another myth that still gets around: *it is a kind of over reliance on the bootstrap philosophy.* There are those who still feel that if the Negro is to rise out of poverty . . . discrimination and segregation, he must do it all by himself. . . . They never stop to realize the debt that they owe a people who were kept in slavery two hundred and forty-four years. In 1863 the Negro was told that he was free as a result of the Emancipation Proc-

lamation. . . . But he was not given any land to make that freedom meaningful. . . . It simply said, "You're free," and it left him there penniless, illiterate, not knowing what to do. And the irony of it all is that *at the same time the nation failed to do anything for the Black man, through an act of Congress it was giving away millions of acres of land in the West and the Midwest.* Which meant that it was willing to undergird its White peasants from Europe with an economic floor. . . . It's all right to tell a man to lift himself by his own bootstraps, but *it is a cruel jest to say to a bootless man that he ought to lift himself by his own bootstraps.* We must come to see that the roots of racism are very deep in our country, and there must be something positive and massive in order to get rid of all the effects of racism and the tragedies of racial injustice.[14]

The American affinity for the bootstrap mentality is in many ways admirable. I fully agree that color-courageous disciples should avoid fostering a mindset of never-ending victimhood and helplessness among people of color. That will not help anyone. We all have the power and the responsibility to make progress regardless of our circumstances. Furthermore, we don't want to undermine the benefits of **meritocracy**—which, when functioning rightly, rewards everyone on the basis of merit and skill.

Yet the issue, as King put it, is *overreliance* on the bootstrap mentality. As it turns out, God often provides for a community through the members' mutual reliance on one another. When there is a special need, some parts of the body may indeed benefit from special attention. We are all called to sacrifice for the sake of building beloved community.

Maybe you now find yourself in agreement with the idea that it is good for disciples to willingly sacrifice for the sake of building beloved community. But what does that look like? More is coming on this, especially in chapter 10 in our discussion on "true" fasting. There, we will look at tangible ways to willingly leverage or sacrifice the various forms of power that we have been given, for God's glory and for the sake of beloved community.

PULL YOURSELF UP BY THE BOOTSTRAPS

Munchausen pulls himself out of a swamp by his hair

The phrase *pull yourself up by your own bootstraps* is sometimes attributed to a German story about a man named Baron Munchausen who pulls himself out of a mire by his own hair. Not only is it a ridiculous story, but it doesn't even have anything to do with boots!

GO AND DO LIKEWISE

I have a friend who once took a survey of more than one hundred evangelical churches and organizations—most of them well-known—to compare their statements of faith. **Evangelicals** are Christians of all ethnic backgrounds who take the Bible seriously and believe in Jesus Christ as Savior and Lord. To his surprise, none of the evangelical statements of faith that my friend reviewed contained the language of love.[15] He reflects:

> We Evangelicals have not rejected love; we have just forgotten to include it in our conversations, mission plans, statements of faith, and theological reflections. That's unfortunate. To move forward, we need to put a priority on the presence of love in our churches, organizations, educational institutions, hearts, and actions. It's not sufficient to *assume* that we love God, each other, and our global neighbors. We need to think about it, talk about it, preach it, practice it, and put it in the center in everything we do.[16]

Love is our beginning. Love is our way. Love must be the end of all our striving. And, as always, Jesus must be both our inspiration and our model for love.

**Love is our beginning. Love is our way.
Love must be the end of all our striving.**

I find this fascinating: When Jesus was asked to illustrate love, he painted a cross-racial picture. A Jewish expert in the law once asked Jesus about what love really looks like, and in response, Jesus told a surprisingly scandalous story about the crossing of an ethnic divide (Luke 10:25–37). While both the Jewish priest and the Jewish scribe passed by the victimized man on the street, it was the Samaritan who stopped and loved by having "compassion" (Luke 10:33, ESV). To have compassion is to *suffer with*: *com-* ("with") plus *-passion* ("suffer"). The word implies a strong, gut-level connection with suffering along with a commitment to alleviate it.

That is the essence of beloved community: a colorful community whose diverse members suffer *and* rejoice together by way of the courage that God provides. It is also why Jesus ended his surprising parable on cross-racial love with these simple words: "Go and do likewise" (Luke 10:37).

THINK ABOUT IT

1. How would you describe beloved community in your own words? When have you enjoyed experiences of beloved community in your own life?

2. Why is fear such a powerful obstacle to love? And how do you think "perfect love drives out fear" (1 John 4:18)?

3. How would you describe agape love to someone else? What would it look like for you to grow in agape love?

4. What is solidarity, and why does love call for solidarity?

5. Explain in your own words the difference between equity and equality.

PART THREE

COLOR-COURAGEOUS SPIRITUAL PRACTICES

We have now come to an important stop along our color-courageous discipleship journey. So let's talk about where we've been and where we're going next.

In part 2, we recovered four discipleship paradigms that can help us more clearly comprehend how a color-courageous posture naturally proceeds from following Jesus Christ. We took an in-depth look at how color-courageous discipleship rediscovers discipleship as awakening, wardrobe change, inner healing, and beloved community.

Yet to grow as color-courageous disciples, we don't just need paradigm shifts. We also need *spiritual practices*. We have said that at its core, racism is a spiritual problem that requires spiritual solutions. We can pursue those spiritual solutions with the help of spiritual practices, also known as spiritual disciplines. Notice the relationship between the words *discipline* and *disciple*. Without spiritual disciplines, disciples are left to dismantle racism by their own strength alone. But *with* spiritual disciplines, color-courageous discipleship can become an intimate journey with

Christ. Spiritual practices are the means of grace that God has provided so that we might access his infinite strength.

In the end, spiritual practices enable us to be transformed so that we can transform the world. But here's the thing: For this transformation to happen, it's not enough to simply *do* spiritual practices; what matters even more is *how* we do them.

It's not enough to simply do spiritual practices; what matters even more is how we do them.

Consider the Pharisees: They were exceedingly faithful when it came to doing spiritual practices. Yet even as the Pharisees did these practices, *there was something about how they did them that served to perpetuate injustice rather than dismantle it.* This is why Jesus said: "Woe to you, teachers of the law and Pharisees, you hypocrites! You give a tenth of your spices—mint, dill and cumin. But you have neglected the more important matters of the law—justice, mercy and faithfulness. You should have practiced the latter, without neglecting the former" (Matthew 23:23).

Consider also institutional slavery in America, Nazism in Germany, and apartheid in South Africa. All three of these legalized racist systems somehow thrived in well-established "Christian" cultures. How can this be? How is it possible to be Christian . . . yet also racist? Faithful Southern Christian slaveholders read their Bibles, prayed, donated to the church, and faithfully worshipped at church every Sunday. So what happened? What went wrong?

Our final example comes from Rwanda. The Rwandan Civil War of 1994 was fundamentally a conflict between warring ethnic groups. After the conflict, this is what Ugandan-born theologian Emmanuel Katongole said when he came upon a destroyed baptismal font in a church:

[The altar] bears the scars of being hacked by machetes, and the church was littered with thousands of bones of people who were killed. You couldn't find a more strange and ironic and tragic image than that: a common baptism surrounded by killing in the name of Hutu and Tutsi.[1]

Yet again, we see this pattern: Rwanda is a primarily Christian country with over 90 percent of Rwandans identifying as Christians. So how was it possible for ethnic and tribal hatred to so perniciously infect its people? Or as Emmanuel Katongole puts it, how could their spiritual practices be "so shallow that they left the blood of tribalism untouched by the water of baptism"?[2]

So we come full circle to this thought: What matters is not only *that we do* spiritual practices as followers of Jesus. What may matter even more is *how we do them*. Are we practicing spiritual disciplines in ways that

- strip our hearts of racism and inspire us to advance God's mission in holistic ways?
- open our eyes to the riches of the technicolor text of the Scriptures?
- equip us to name the cultural lenses that we bring to our Bible reading?
- encourage us to process pain and racial trauma well, especially through lament?
- prompt us to name and uproot the unconscious biases of our hearts?
- move us to cross geographic and cultural boundaries?
- incline us toward empathy for others, especially those on the margins?
- influence us to understand our power so that we might better leverage it for others?

- empower us to carry our cross with Christ in every part of our lives, including race?
- foster within us the godly courage we need to dismantle racism and build beloved community for a lifetime?

Beloved friends, our spiritual practices have so much potential to cultivate color-courageous discipleship! *But if we want to realize the potential of our spiritual practices, we need to do them differently.* That is why, in part 3, we will discover how we can practice four common spiritual disciples in uncommon ways. Two of these practices may be more familiar to you (Bible reading and prayer), while the other two may be less familiar (pilgrimage and fasting "for real").

Using these practices as examples, we will seek to understand how we can live into all our spiritual practices in color-courageous ways. If we want to faithfully follow Jesus, dismantle racism, and build beloved community, we need spiritual practices that will truly transform *us*—heart, soul, and mind—as we seek to transform our world.

READ (IN LIVING COLOR)

Rediscover the Technicolor Text

I am not myself by myself.

—EUGENE PETERSON, *CHRIST PLAYS IN TEN THOUSAND PLACES*

When I first heard the news about the Lausanne Movement for World Evangelization as a seminary student, I knew I had to find a way to get invited to one of its global gatherings. This is despite the fact that I was still quite young . . . and quite broke! Founded by Billy Graham, the Lausanne Movement is known for its commitment to mobilize "the whole church to take the whole gospel to the whole world," and it has played a meaningful role in shaping global missions over the past century. Miraculously, both my husband and I applied, were accepted, and then swiftly raised the financial support we needed to go. With a diaper bag and Snap-N-Go stroller in hand, we toted our wide-eyed eight-month-old right along with us. In the end, Cape Town 2010 hosted more than four thousand leaders from 198 countries and was hailed as "the most representative gathering of Christian leaders in the 2,000-year history of the Christian movement."[1]

My most vivid memories will always be of the opening night.

Together with people from myriad tribes, tongues, and nations, brothers and sisters from diverse African nations and cultural backgrounds led us in awe-inspiring worship. Just as we all experience our smallness before the roar of the endless sea, I was stunned by my own smallness in comparison to the boundless breadth and depth of the church—both gorgeously global and inexhaustibly colorful. What would it look like to be enriched by our incomparably colorful church in my everyday discipleship practices too?

Our journey in Christ will be richer to the extent that it reflects the beautiful words of the Nicene Creed, an ancient Christian statement of faith: "We believe in one holy catholic and apostolic church." We get to follow Jesus together with the church across time ("apostolic") and around the world ("catholic"). Unfortunately, most of us are missing out. Our discipleship consists of bland monochromatic snack food instead of the rich banquet that God intends.

What does that mean when it comes to reading the Bible? Color-courageous disciples take a different approach: They seek to read the Bible in living color, both to glean more riches from the Bible and to attain wisdom for bringing racial shalom to the world.

Reading the Bible in living color means we read the Bible with cultural awareness in two major ways. First, it means that we understand that our own culture impacts the way we read and understand the Bible. We do not approach the Bible as a blank slate. So, when we read, we seek to ask: *How does my own culture impact my Bible reading?*

> *Reading the Bible in living color means reading God's Word in an antiracist, color-courageous way.*

Second, it means that we work hard to understand the Bible's culture—which is way different from our own! Reading the

Bible in living color also means asking: *How does learning the Bible's culture help me understand the Bible better?* Because we are confined to our own time and place, thousands of years away from biblical contexts, we have to understand that we usually have a hard time imagining Bible settings accurately.

Reading the Bible in living color means reading God's Word in an antiracist, color-courageous way. Rather than tainting our reading of Scripture with the racial and cultural assumptions that we bring to the text, we are free to better understand its original meaning and to more fully enjoy the colorful riches of God's Word.

DISCOVER YOUR OWN CULTURAL CONTEXT

Let's begin with our first question: *How does my own culture impact my Bible reading?* You know, whenever we open a book, we most often see a mirror! What I mean is that we have a tendency to read our assumptions and experiences—our own "culture"—into the text. Now here's the thing: None of us is *without* culture. Given that we cannot remove our culture any more than we can remove our DNA, we can and should become more aware of what our culture *is*. If we do not, misreading the Bible is the inevitable result. There are now many great resources out there about this, by the way, like the book *Misreading Scripture with Western Eyes: Removing Cultural Blinders to Better Understand the Bible.*[2]

Let's consider a few examples. Did you know that many predominantly White Christian churches have their own culture too? Sometimes, we make the mistake of thinking that only churches of color—which some call "ethnic" churches—have "culture." Not true! One sociologist by the name of Michael Emerson has done lots of research specifically on White **evangelical** Christian culture.[3] He discovered that an element of the culture is **individualism.** When your culture is individualistic, it means that you usually think "me" first rather than "we." That's not necessarily a bad thing: For example, it probably means that you take your personal spiritual life very seriously, which is fantastic. However, when taken too far, individualism can cause people to miss important things when they read the Bible. For example, when you read a command in the Bible, who do you think it is addressing? I'm guessing that you often think that the command addresses you (singular "you"—the reader) rather than the whole group that you're are part of (plural "you"—your whole church or youth group).

EVANGELICALS

What are evangelical Christians? According to the National Association of Evangelicals (NAE):

Evangelicals take the Bible seriously and believe in Jesus Christ as Savior and Lord. The term "evangelical" comes from the Greek word *euangelion*, meaning "the good news" or the "gospel." Thus, the evangelical faith focuses on the "good news" of salvation brought to sinners by Jesus Christ. Evangelicals are a vibrant and diverse group including believers found in many churches, denominations and nations.[4]

Based on this definition, would you call yourself an evangelical? Why or why not?

Let's take the example of Isaiah 1:17: "Learn to do good; seek justice, correct oppression; bring justice to the fatherless, plead the widow's cause" (ESV). Those reading this in an individualistic culture are likely to think: *How can I learn to do good and seek jus-*

tice? *Perhaps I can read more books or volunteer with a local ministry.* And that would be fantastic! However, it's vital to understand that all the verbs in this verse are actually *plural.* They are meant for a group. Consider how it would change the meaning for you if you read it like this: "*As a group,* learn to do good, seek justice, and correct oppression." It's pretty different, don't you think?

In individualistic cultures, disciples do not tend to ask questions like: *What would it look like to resist racism not only as individuals but also as a group? What responsibility does my whole youth group or church have to dismantle racism together?*

Have you read the Bible story of Achan, whose entire family was punished for one man's "individual" sin? (You can find the story in Joshua 7.) Disciples who are in individualistic cultures tend to be really confused by this story! They wonder: *Why was Achan's entire family punished for one man's sin? That isn't fair!* But here's the thing: Although "Achan's family . . . did not do the stealing . . . they helped him become the kind of man who would steal."[5] If you are born into a family that has a pattern of sinning in certain ways (or repeatedly tolerating certain sins), you are more likely to do the same thing. So what does that mean when it comes to racism? Disciples in individualistic cultures tend to see racism as an individual problem. These disciples try to fix racism by identifying and uprooting *individual people* in a system—that is, finding the "bad apples"—rather than understanding how the *whole system* might be contributing to the problem. But in order to defeat racism, we've got to do both!

A second characteristic of White evangelical culture is *relationalism.* In relational cultures, personal relationships are the key. That means that if we are having a problem of some kind, we tend to think first about what might be amiss with our relationships. Once again, this is a wonderful strength. For example, evangelical Christians are not satisfied with religious rituals—for us, a personal relationship with God is paramount. And it is! On the other hand, relational culture can also cause us to view huge social problems—like widespread racial inequity—as simply a problem of poor relationships. But the truth is that in order to deal with racial inequity, we need to do more than make friends with people of other races. We also need to address systemic issues such as unfair systems, structures, and policies.

Disciples in relational cultures prefer to resist racism by getting people together, pursuing unity, or developing cross-racial friendships. They prefer conversations about racial *reconciliation* rather than racial *justice*. But to resist racism in a truly restorative way, color-courageous disciples seek not only to repair relationships; they also seek ways to tangibly repair whatever else has been broken. Take the story of Zacchaeus: After his encounter with Jesus, Zacchaeus showed true repentance not only because he apologized but because he made **restitution**. To make restitution is to restore something that was taken or lost. Zacchaeus exclaimed: "Look, Lord! Here and now I give half of my possessions to the poor, and if I have cheated anybody out of anything, I will pay back four times the amount" (Luke 19:8). This act of spiritual repentance, generously demonstrated through tangible restitution, is what prompted Jesus to proclaim with delight: "Today salvation has come to this house" (verse 9).

We find another brilliant example soon after the birth of the church in Acts 6: "In those days when the number of disciples was increasing, the Hellenistic Jews among them complained against the Hebraic Jews because their widows were being overlooked in the daily distribution of food" (Acts 6:1). The Hellenistic Jews and the Hebraic Jews were both *Jesus-followers,* but they came from *different ethnic cultures.* Now remember: At Pentecost, just a few chapters earlier in Acts 2, God had just clearly demonstrated his fiery desire for a church of diverse disciples. Yet soon after, we see a painful example of ethnic conflict!

In this story, we see yet another example of the **intention vs. impact dilemma.** It was probably not the *intention* of the Hebraic Jews to mistreat the Hellenistic Jews. These were all

God-fearing people. Nevertheless, ethnic mistreatment was exactly the *impact* of their existing systems, policies, and power structures. We learn color-courageous discipleship by seeing how the Twelve—all Hebraic Jews—responded when the Hellenistic Jews complained. They did not deny that there was a problem, drag their feet, blame the victims, or tell them to pull themselves up by their bootstraps. Instead, they took action to change the system so that biblical equity was the result. In fact, the Twelve changed the power structure itself, raising up Hellenistic leaders to oversee the food distribution. What was the result? "The word of God spread," and the "number of disciples in Jerusalem increased rapidly" (Acts 6:7). That is the power of color-courageous discipleship at work!

The truth is that our own culture has a profound impact on how we read, understand, and apply the Bible. If you think you don't have a culture—which is often true of dominant-culture disciples—that's an urgent flag that you have work to do! *What's more, if your culture is dominant, you are more likely to be blind to what your culture actually is.* This is why White-culture disciples, in particular, can perhaps benefit more than anyone else from self-reflection. That being said, color-courageous readers from all backgrounds must constantly work to grow in their awareness of the cultural biases they bring to the biblical text.

One more thing: Reading with particular cultural lenses also inclines us to read *particular parts* of the Bible more than other parts. I was reminded of this in a powerful way when I visited the innovative Museum of the Bible in Washington, D.C.

The most memorable exhibit for me was found in the museum's "African American Experience" wing. Behind a large glass pane, I spotted a copy of the Slave Bible—a "Bible" produced specifically for use by slaves. The story of the exodus of Israelite slaves from Egypt was removed, as were major passages that talk about equality between groups of people, such as Galatians 3:28: "There is neither Jew nor Gentile, neither slave nor free, nor is there male and female, for you are all one in Christ Jesus." The book of Revelation—which, as we know, depicts a diverse family of disciples before the throne of God—was also left out. This supposed "Bible" was not *holy* precisely because it was not *whole*. And here's the thing: While the slave *owners* might have possessed their own *complete* copies of the Bible, the Slave Bible nevertheless reveals that in their cultural context, they clearly preferred certain parts of their Bibles to others.

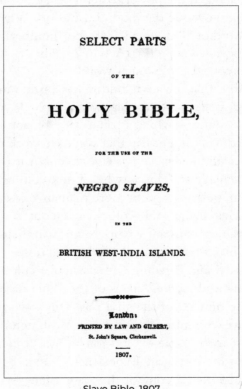

Slave Bible, 1807

As disciples, we are actually not so different today. We affirm the Bible as our foundation for discipleship, but we also prefer to

spend most of our time in certain parts. Perhaps we do this because, just like those who created the Slave Bible, we would rather
avoid certain parts that make us uncomfortable or challenge our
way of life. This tendency to read selectively is cultural too.

We now move to our second question: *How does learning the
Bible's culture help me to understand it better?*

DISCOVER THE BIBLE'S CULTURES

It was a normal Sunday morning in Birmingham in September
1963 when four little girls clothed in colorful dresses made their
way to services at Sixteenth Street Baptist Church. I imagine
them, like most kids, giggling and fidgeting during Sunday
school in the church basement through Bible lessons and gospel
songs. After class, they gather to change into white choir robes.
As they run back upstairs to bless the congregation with song,
their final awareness is a brilliant flash of burning light.

The Ku Klux Klan proudly took responsibility for the explo-
sion of the nineteen sticks of dynamite that killed Addie Mae,
Carol, Carole, and Cynthia. The brutal blast mutilated one of
the girls so badly that she could only be identified by her clothing. The bombing was a major motivating event for the Civil
Rights Movement.

In the aftermath of that horrific event, people saw a very
strange sight. At the time, Sixteenth Street Baptist Church was
flanked by a series of beautiful stained-glass windows. One of
the most startling images to emerge from the wreckage was a
damaged window that featured a faceless White Jesus, his visage
perfectly blown away with eerie precision. The strange sight has
prompted me (and others) to wonder: *In a Black church that was
nearly destroyed by a White terrorist group, isn't it a little strange that
Jesus is also depicted as a White person?*

In Western contexts, when we read the narratives of Jesus in

Sixteenth Street Baptist Church
BIRMINGHAM, ALA., PUBLIC LIBRARY ARCHIVES

the Bible, we tend to imagine him with white skin. But when and how did Jesus "become" White?

Perhaps the most famous portrait of Christ was created in 1923 by the artist Warner Sallman, a member of my own denomination—the Evangelical Covenant Church, known then as the Swedish Covenant Church. Originally, Sallman created a charcoal portrait of Christ to grace the cover of our denominational magazine, *The Covenant Companion*. People loved it! In fact, the "popularity of the cover was so great that requests for reprints streamed in after all 7,000 copies of the magazine were sold."[6] Later, in 1940, Sallman was commissioned to paint this portrait of Jesus in full color as a gift to the graduating class of North Park Theological Seminary. This resulted in the now-famous portrait of a European Christ looking heavenward with blue eyes and flowing hair. Some refer to it as the "Swedish" Jesus. This is certainly understandable given that the painting originated in a Swedish American Christian context.

Sallman's inspired work has brought joy and comfort to countless people—including to scores of American servicemen who were given pocket-sized reproductions of Sallman's Christ during World War II.[7] The painting has been called "the best-known American artwork of the 20th century" and can be found all around the world.[8] There are more reprints of this White Jesus in circulation than there are people in the United States. In fact, it's considered to be the most reproduced image ever, having been reprinted over one billion times![9]

We tend to imagine Jesus in our own racial and cultural image. We do this out of a deep desire to relate to Jesus—and that is a wonderful thing. You can now find images of Jesus portrayed in every ethnicity—just google it! At the same time, portraying Jesus in our image can also have unintended consequences—yet another example of the intention vs. impact dilemma. The *intention* behind these images is usually good. At the same time, depicting Jesus in our image can also have an unintended *impact*. In the words of my colleague Paul Robinson, executive minister of Love Mercy Do Justice for the Evangelical Covenant Church, Eurocentric depictions like these have caused many to link "Jesus with the very real experience of racism at the hands of some white people and institutions."[10]

What do we know about what Jesus looked like? We do know that "the earliest depictions of Jews, which date from the 3rd Century, are—as far as can be determined—dark-skinned. . . . 'The safest thing is to talk about Jesus as "a man of colour."'"[11] In *The Historical Jesus: An Essential Guide,* James H. Charlesworth writes that Jesus's skin was "most likely dark brown and sun-tanned."[12] Just imagine: What if the vast majority of our depictions of Christ—in books, posters, frescoes, and stained-glass windows the world over—portrayed a more historically accurate Brown, or even "dark brown," Jesus? What difference would that make for our shared perception and treatment of Black and Brown people today?

Given the racial challenges that we face today, it is vital to comprehend—not only with our *minds* but also with our *hearts*—

that the main character of the Bible was not a White person.
Jesus was Jewish, a marginalized and oppressed minority of the
Roman Empire, and most likely one with brown skin.

The Covenant Companion cover,
February 1924

When we read Jesus in living color—as he actually was—we
more deeply understand that "Jesus identifies with the oppressed
and that the experience of marginalized people is not foreign to
God."[13] Today, I am grateful that the Evangelical Covenant
Church now *excels* when it comes to multiethnic diversity—but
it has taken us many years of intentionality to get here.

When we read the Bible in living color, we perceive Jesus (and
all other Bible characters) in their full vibrance and reality. As we
do, new insights will emerge that enrich our understanding of the
text, our faith, and our capacity to build beloved community.

READ WITH COLORFUL COMMUNITY

My friend Max Lee, professor of New Testament at North Park
Theological Seminary, has taught and refined a course for years

called "Intercultural Readings of the Bible." Originally prompted by students of color at the seminary, the course explores an **intercultural** approach to reading the Bible that results in mutual insight and transformation.

Although the Word of God does not change, the same text can result in fresh insights when read from different vantage points. This is exciting! Bible reading in a colorful community enriches us by means of exchanging **community cultural wealth,** the unique contributions that each culture can make to the world. These contributions can include knowledge, values, skills, artifacts, wisdom accumulated from common experiences, and much more. As we have learned, ethnicity is a God-ordained cultural identity that God delights in as a means of bringing glory to himself and enrichment to his kingdom. This is exactly what we see in the biblical vision of the new creation where every culture brings unique treasures into the kingdom of God (Isaiah 60:1–14; Revelation 21:24–26). Thankfully, we don't have to wait until the new creation to experience these riches.

Indigenous Bible readers like Randy Woodley, for example, draw us to the connection between discipleship and creation. In *Shalom and the Community of Creation: An Indigenous Vision,* he explores how we can experience deep well-being not only when we are reconciled with God and fellow humans, but also when we are reconciled with all creation—the earth, the animals, the forests, and the environment.[14] Indigenous readings like his remind us that all creation is groaning under the weight of a curse of our own doing (Romans 8:22). They also remind us that disciples can become ambassadors of holistic shalom as we steward creation with care, as we worship with creation as we see in the psalms, and as we receive insight from creation—as Jesus taught us when he directed us to learn from sparrows, lilies, vines, and even water.

James Cone, a Black reader of the Bible, wrote *The Cross and the Lynching Tree,* in which he makes some truly striking connections between Jesus's suffering on the cross and the suffering of Black people on countless American lynching trees.[15] Like countless Blacks who were lynched in America, Jesus, too, was unjustly accused, falsely condemned, maliciously mocked, and hung to die on a tree. Yet he did so "for the joy set before him" (Hebrews 12:2)—and then experienced resurrection from the dead. Today, many Black readers also remind the church that joy is an act of resistance and that there is always the possibility of life beyond death.

My colleague Dominique Gilliard, author of *Rethinking Incarceration,* is another Black Bible reader who makes eye-opening comparisons between criminal justice in the Bible and criminal justice today.[16] Jesus and the disciples suffered injustices within the criminal justice system, just as many people of color do today. Jesus was imprisoned by a biased judiciary. Although he was innocent, he received the death sentence. And remember: Many of the apostles and disciples "did time"—entire books of the Bible were written by convicted criminals! When we remember these events, it prompts new questions: How are we identifying and addressing unfairness and bias in our criminal justice systems today? Do we paint all incarcerated people with the same brush? Are we making restorative investments in prisons, understanding them to be fertile fields and even launching pads for ministry? Did you know, for example, that incarcerated people are now partnering with free churches in creative and beautiful ways—making disciples and even planting churches behind bars? It is breathtakingly beautiful.[17]

Latino/a readers have drawn attention to the fact that Jesus could be considered, in modern parlance, both an immigrant and a refugee. Some great examples of authors who have done this are Justo González (author of *Santa Biblia: The Bible Through Hispanic Eyes*) and Robert Chao Romero (author of *Brown Church*).[18] Just as many immigrants attempt entry into the United States to flee violence or poverty, so too did Joseph, Mary, and

Jesus abruptly migrate to Egypt to escape violence in Israel. In fact, our generation has seen some of the largest refugee migrations in human history. To what extent can we recognize God in the immigrants among us—many of whom are Christian too?

Flight into Egypt, Eugène Girardet

We receive even more colorful insights from Scripture as we read with the global church. For example, Indian readers help us to see how Christianity could thrive in a society where there are multiple religions. There are African and Asian readers who might help us to understand what it means to live out our faith not only with our present community but also with our community of faithful ancestors, becoming more mindful of the "great cloud of witnesses" that surrounds us (Hebrews 12:1). South Korean readers, with their long tradition of intensive early morning prayer, can teach us to enjoy the benefits of awakening the dawn in worship (Psalm 57:8; 108:2) and "pray[ing] in the Spirit on all occasions" (Ephesians 6:18). There are so many more examples that we could share.

Of course, it is important that we do not overgeneralize when it comes to racial and cultural groups. Although there are often commonly shared characteristics in a group, each member is still a unique individual. The main takeaway here is that the wider and more diverse your reading community is, the richer and more accurate your understanding of the Bible will be. How diverse are the voices speaking into your life? For example, how colorful are the authors on your bookshelf?

Reading with a colorful community highlights the importance of **decentering** one's own culture—not to diminish one's own culture, but to acknowledge that each culture is just one among many in a rich tapestry of unique cultural perspectives. No culture is at the center—only Jesus is at the center! And we need one another to understand Jesus better. And that is just as God would have it, for we are creatures designed for community. Color-courageous disciples read in living color to get more of God and to fulfill more of God's good purposes in the world.

LOVE IN LIVING COLOR

When I worked on Wall Street, the work hours were brutal. Under my desk, I stored a pillow and blankets for snoozing at work. It was challenging to maintain a semblance of spiritual life, but I was creative.

One day, I found an empty conference room and started to pace and pray aloud vigorously. Suddenly, my friend Maurice opened the door. He gave me a bemused look, shut the door, and swiftly vanished. I chuckled, knowing I'd have some explaining to do. Later he messaged me: "Hey, so . . . what were you doing up there?!" My response: "Yup, you caught me. I'm not crazy, I promise. I was just talking to the Man Upstairs!"

In the end, I was grateful for the kerfuffle because it launched an ongoing spiritual conversation. Maurice had graduated at the top of his class from Morehouse College, one of the most prestigious HBCUs (historically Black colleges and universities). He was gently intimidating and undeniably brilliant. He was also firmly opposed to the Christian faith. At lunch one day, he asked me point-blank: "Michelle, how can you seriously believe this stuff? Don't you get that Christianity has been an oppressive tool for hundreds of years?" As we have learned, there is truth to accusations like these.[19] Christian "discipleship" for Blacks has included oppressive tools like the Slave Bible.

But as I prayed, a light bulb came on: *I shifted from sharing Jesus in a "color-blind" way to sharing Jesus in living color.* I said: "Maurice, you are right. Christianity has been co-opted as a tool of oppression—especially with the Black community. And that breaks my heart. But you know what? I like to stay focused on Jesus himself—who he actually was, what he said and did. You remember, right? He was also a marginalized and oppressed minority. Most likely a Brown one. He can relate." At that point, I could see the lights turning on for Maurice, too, in subtle sparks of insight and curiosity about the true Jesus. It was a turning point in his willingness to reconsider the Christian faith.

It is projected that by 2045, the majority of Americans will be people of color.[20] Younger generations like yours have already surpassed this milestone—you are the most multiethnic generation ever! Now and long into the future, reading *and* loving in living color will be key to reaching people for Jesus Christ.

———

Many have heard about the tragedy of the four little girls at Sixteenth Street Baptist Church, but far fewer have heard about what came after. Disciples of Jesus mobilized on a global level to restore what had been broken—including the stained-glass windows.

Across the ocean in Wales, a Christian artist began to fashion a brand-new stained-glass window as a restorative gift for the church. Often ironically referred to as *The Wales Window,* it portrays a brown-skinned Jesus on a cross. Now, don't miss his hands: Jesus's right hand is defiantly resisting injustice while his left hand is extending forgiveness. It's the very posture of color-courageous discipleship—resisting racism while building beloved community. The window is accompanied by the words "You do it to me," based on Matthew 25:40: "Truly I tell you, whatever you did for one of the least of these brothers and sisters of mine, you did for me." Today, the church lives on as a thriving community and beacon for justice and hope.

The Wales Window, Sixteenth Street Baptist Church, Birmingham, Alabama, 2010

PHOTO BY CAROL M. HIGHSMITH,
LIBRARY OF CONGRESS

The point, of course, is not that we'll fix all our racial challenges by replacing our images of a White Jesus with a Jesus that is African, Latino, or Indigenous. The point is that when we revisit the Bible in living color—including Jesus himself—we will be blessed with new insight. We may be reminded, for example, that Jesus was a marginalized person who held up even more marginalized peoples as role models. No doubt, this will impact how we engage marginalized communities today. As we read the Bible in living color, we see more clearly that God is at work in all cultures and peoples—and so all should be honored as exemplars of the royal image of God.

THINK ABOUT IT

1. Have you ever experienced Christianity in a culture different from yours or visited a church of a different ethnic group? What was that like? What did you learn or experience?

2. Visit any art museum and you will likely see Jesus has overwhelmingly been portrayed throughout much of history as a White male. What difference do you think it makes, for people of all races, when they really comprehend that Jesus was not a White person?

3. How would you explain this statement to someone else: "If your culture is dominant, you are more likely to be blind to what your culture actually is."

4. How would you explain to someone else what it means to "read the Bible in living color"?

5. If you could study the Bible together with disciples of a different ethnic or cultural background from your own, who would you choose to study with and why?

PRAY (IN THE RAW)

Lament Your Way to Faith, Hope, and Love

Pain insists upon being attended to. God whispers to us
in our pleasures, speaks in our conscience, but shouts in
our pain: it is His megaphone to rouse a deaf world.
—C. S. LEWIS, *THE PROBLEM OF PAIN*

It's a Tuesday morning in September, and I'm at work, gearing up for the day. I look up from my desk and see a most curious thing outside the window: a waterfall of white documents showering from the sky. They are fluttering every which way like confused butterflies. I wonder: *What is this? Has a Xerox machine exploded somewhere?*

At that moment, I was sitting on the seventeenth floor of my company's skyscraper in downtown Manhattan. After studying international business in college, I had landed a fancy job as an investment banker at Goldman Sachs. I had launched my career at one of the most prestigious banks on Wall Street! Many of my classmates, upon hearing the news, simply raised their eyebrows in astonishment.

Frankly, I was astonished too. As a woman of color, the odds had been stacked against me. Women of color, and Black women in particular, have long suffered poor rates of hiring, pay, and promotion in the corporate world. There were very few people at Goldman Sachs who looked like me. Nevertheless, by God's grace, I had made it!

Summer training was done. The date was September 11, 2001—my second day on assignment. I had not been at my desk long that morning when paper started to rain down from the sky. Of course, we soon learned that much more was going on than an exploding photocopier. It was terrorism that had exploded into our world. Mayhem and confusion descended. In one moment, I was desperate to get out of there, wondering: *Would our building be next?* In the next moment, I was desperate to stay, too scared to go outside. The day had suddenly turned to night, and the air was choked with thick, putrid, and possibly toxic smoke.

At some point, we were given masks and urged to vacate the area. When I walked outside, I felt like I was emerging from a spaceship, just landed on a faraway planet. *Everything* was cloaked in ghostly white ash—buildings, cars, and people. Quiet . . . everything was eerily quiet in the city that always speaks and *never* sleeps. Every phone cut off. No honking taxis, no screeching subways. The people, too, were staggering around in silence. And the smell, I will simply never forget the stench—unnatural, metallic, and foul. I can smell it now.

At the time, I lived in Brooklyn, miles away from my office. But like everyone else, I could only get home that day by walking. So I started the trek—first in heels, then in bare feet. It was surreal to cross over the Brooklyn Bridge, just one dot in a sea of stunned people, the city still aflame behind us. I was terrified that a third or fourth plane would come. I imagined it smashing into the bridge and causing me to tumble to my death in the cold, dark water below. At that moment, this thought bolted into my mind: *If I had to meet God right now, would I be ready?* I had a relationship with Jesus, yes. Yet I had pursued many of my career choices primarily for me rather than for him. Much of my life had been blighted by bitterness about having *less*. Black women always seemed to have *less*. But I was determined that my story would be different. So, I had decided to chase after earthly treasures, come what may. I wanted to quell my insecurities once and for all.

To be clear, a financial career *is* a God-honoring career choice for many people. But, in my heart, I knew that banking was not for me. I didn't even *like* what I was doing every day. What would it look like for me to truly trust God not only with my career . . . but with everything?

On 9/11, I felt a clear nudge from God to go back to the drawing board of my life. But before I could even think about doing that, God directed me to go on a walk with him through the valley of the shadow of death. In the days that followed, I was plagued by trauma and grief. It was the sheer randomness of it all that made it so disturbing. I was tormented by the endless loop on television of people jumping from the burning inferno of the Twin Towers to an unimaginably gruesome death—some of whom, I was certain, had to be followers of Jesus. Imagine it: One moment, you're at work bright and early, groggily consuming a cup of coffee and making plans for the day. In the blink of an eye, you are deciding between burning alive or jumping from a window to your death. I just couldn't wrap my mind around it. Sometime after, the towers were memorialized for the entire city in an art installation called the *Tribute in Light*. It featured two towering shafts of light that reached straight up to the heavens. But really, what kind of God were they reaching out to? What kind of God was *I* reaching out to?

I plunged into depression. I began meeting regularly with a deacon from my church. I shed countless tears. I was filled with rage as I considered not only this event but all the other horrific things that God allows to happen. I agonized: *What kind of God allows pain like this?* I cried out to God and begged him to show

The 9/11 *Tribute in Light*
PHOTO BY U.S. AIR FORCE, DENISE GOULD

me the way through . . . because I couldn't see one. And then he did.

I had a dream that I was running through a deep forest. I knew that I was on some kind of mission for Jesus in this place. But for some reason, I was being pursued by people who wanted to kill me. I was terrified. And I knew with clarity: *This is it. This is the end. I'm going to lose my life.* Suddenly, a door appeared in midair. It opened to perfection, beauty, and radiant light. Pastel flower petals burst from the door. Just as my attackers came upon me, I ran through the door—which then promptly vanished.

I woke up with a start, awash with relief. I knew two things with complete certainty: One, my worst fear had come to pass. Going through that door meant that I had died. Two, going through that door also meant that God had saved me. It meant that I was home at last, safe and secure, and about to embark upon a new forever-adventure with God. My soul flooded with gratitude and joy. *Okay, Jesus,* I thought, *I got the message. I'm always in your hands, no matter what.*

I share my 9/11 experience with you not because it is about *race* but because it is about *pain*. We cannot deal with one without dealing with the other. Through 9/11 and its aftermath, I endured some of the most excruciating pain of my life. My antiracist journey, too, has meant dealing with excruciating pain—my pain as well as the pain of others. Color-courageous disciples must learn to grapple with racial pain rather than avoid it if they hope to effectively build beloved community. But before we talk specifically about racial pain, let's first return to the Scriptures and understand some things about how pain works in general—as well as the remedy that God has provided.

GOD'S ANTIDOTE FOR PAIN

Pain is pervasive in our fallen world. When pain prompts us to become angry or resentful toward God, our relationship with God becomes distorted. And when we inevitably cause one another pain, our relationships with others become distorted too. And when one *group* causes another group pain, it frustrates the possibility of beloved community.

But here's the amazing thing: God has provided us with an antidote that can transform pain into a spiritual catalyst. That antidote is lament. In the cauldron of our suffering, God invites us to lament, to pray in the raw. At its heart, **lament** is a "prayer in pain that leads to trust."[1] Learning to lament is like learning a new language. It's the language that God has given disciples to talk to him about pain. The language of lament does not come easily, but as we become increasingly fluent in it, we will find that our pain increasingly becomes infused with God-given possibility.

More than ever, we are becoming aware of the racial pain all around us. Yet it is precisely because the contemporary church has tended to avoid pain that we have been ineffective in our racial reconciliation and racial justice efforts. In response, modern-day prophets urge the church to realize that lament is vital, both for personal shalom and for long-lasting racial shalom between groups.

In this chapter, we will examine personal and corporate lament, as well as a third kind—divine lament—and explore how each brims with potential for healing and spiritual growth.

THE GIFT OF PERSONAL LAMENT

Our relationship with God deepens as we increasingly allow ourselves to bring our pain to him: unprocessed, real, and raw. We live in a desperately broken world, a fallen world teeming with pain. Lament is the gift that God has given us to talk to him about that pain. Our human default is to avoid pain, but in lament, we learn to bring our pain to God.

Lament is how we allow God to infuse our pain with possibility. Lament is God's invitation for us to be honest with him and, ultimately, to trust him to work out his good purposes through our pain.

But this is critical: Lament acknowledges that we can't entrust our pain to God unless we've been real with him about it first. We can't entrust our pain to God unless we have taken the risk to be authentic with him about our anger and our disappointment in him for allowing that pain. We can't entrust our pain to God in prayer unless we "pray in the raw."

The book of Psalms is the disciple's prayer book, teaching us what it means to pray in the raw. While most of the Bible is God's Word directed at us, the book of Psalms is our word directed at God. It shows us what it looks like to bring the full range of human emotion to God. The psalms come in all varieties—praise psalms, thanksgiving psalms, royal psalms, and more. But did you know that the largest number of psalms are psalms of lament?

THE DIVERSITY OF PSALMS

The book of Psalms is the Bible's hymnal or songbook. There are a wide variety of psalms meant to reflect the wide variety of human emotions and experiences. Psalms is also the longest book of the Bible! I think that's God's clue to us that it's okay to bring *every* emotion to him, that it is okay to pray in the raw.

PSALM TYPE	SONGS OF . . .
Thanksgiving	Gratitude (18, 30, 40, 92)
Praise	Worship, Celebration (8, 47, 65, 66, 150)
Lamentation	Sorrow (3, 6, 11, 22, 44, 77, 102)
Imprecatory	Anger (35, 55, 109, 137)
Messianic/Royal	Songs to Honor the King (2, 110)

The psalms of lament reveal how we can bring our pain to God in a healthy way. In *Dark Clouds, Deep Mercy,* Mark Vroegop relates his devastating experience in grieving a stillborn child. He describes four movements that he discovered as he immersed himself in the psalms of lament: (1) Turn, (2) Complain, (3) Ask, and (4) Trust.[2] Let's take a brief look at each of these now, specifically in the twenty-second psalm. I encourage you to take a moment to read the psalm now.

Psalm 22 is attributed to King David and written during a time when he felt abandoned by God. Still, David eventually made a conscious decision to *turn* to God in his pain. He asked, "My God, my God, why have you forsaken me?" (verse 1). You, too, always have a choice about whether or not you will turn to God in your pain.

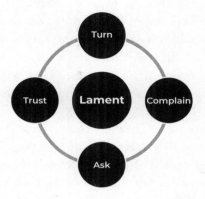

Next, David *complained* before God. He modeled for us the need to *get real,* and he does plenty of it in Psalm 22: "I cry out by day, but you do not answer, by night, but I find no rest" (verse 2). God invites you to be brutally honest with him about your pain because God wants to meet you where you actually are. Think about it: Where else can he meet you? God's desire is to meet you *where you actually are* so that he can comfort you, heal you, walk with you, and guide you toward abundant life.

> *God's desire is to meet you* where you actually are *so that he can comfort you, heal you, walk with you, and guide you toward abundant life.*

The third step in lament is to *ask.* David asked God for many things: "Do not be far from me, for trouble is near" (verse 11). "You are my strength; come quickly to help me" (verse 19). "Rescue me from the mouth of the lions" (verse 21). In our pain, God yearns for us to ask for comfort, hope, and peace.

Being honest about what you *really* want—even if you have asked God for the very same things before—is another opportunity to present your true self to God and grow your relationship with him. In the process of asking, you often will also gain clarity into what would truly be best for you—sometimes it is what you're asking for, and sometimes you'll realize that it's not! And finally, let's not forget that sometimes God will give us *exactly* what we ask for—when the opportunity is right, he delights to do that too (Matthew 7:7; James 4:2)!

The final frontier of lament is *trust*. Trust is our highest expression of love for God. David wrote: "In you our ancestors put their trust; they trusted and you delivered them" (Psalm 22:4). When David wrote prayers like these, his pain had *not* vanished. Nevertheless, he discovered profound peace—and even new-found praise—as he chose to trust in God's greater purposes for his life. And you can too.

In the life of Jesus, we discover a beautiful moment when his own prayerful ask blossomed into prayerful trust. On the night before his death, Jesus lamented. He turned to God and asked to be spared from pain . . . but then he concluded with a declaration of trust: "I want your will to be done, not mine" (Matthew 26:39, NLT). Jesus trusted that if God allowed this pain into his life, then God would certainly work his good purposes through it.

God can take our pain—including our racial pain—and repurpose it to form deep and unshakable faith.

Faith means believing "in advance what will only make sense in reverse."[3] I do not understand why God allowed me to suffer merciless racial trauma as a little girl. I do not understand why God allows systemic inequity to persist. Nor do I understand why God allows heart-rending catastrophes like 9/11 to explode into our lives. What I *do* understand is that the only way forward is *trust*. God can take our pain—including our racial pain—and repurpose it to form deep and unshakable faith.

FAITH LIKE GOLD

Did you know that your faith is priceless to God? Another word for faith is *trust*. What God wants most of all is for you to trust that *he is good* and that *he loves you*—no matter what happens.  When we don't trust God, it leads to trouble. That's what happened in the Garden of Eden. Satan convinced Adam and Eve *not* to trust God but rather to trust Satan—and themselves. That's when mayhem broke loose, because only God knows what is best for us. That is why *discipleship is largely a journey of growing trust in God.* As disciples, we have the opportunity to grow our faith every day and in every circumstance—especially through challenges and hard times. We cannot understand everything about the things we suffer, but one thing we know: "Their purpose is to prove that your faith is genuine. Even gold, which can be destroyed, is tested by fire; and so your faith, which is much more precious than gold, must also be tested, so that it may endure" (1 Peter 1:7, GNT).

THE GRACE OF GROUP LAMENT

To the extent that they learn to process their personal pain through lament, color-courageous disciples will be able to help others process their pain too. As we learned from our chapter on inner healing, healing from pain and trauma of all kinds is vital for the work of antiracism. We are now ready for our next question: *How can lamenting together help us dismantle racism and build beloved community?*

Lamenting together forges loving connections between communities as we weep with those who weep and rejoice with those who rejoice (Romans 12:15). We have seen that *solidarity* is vital to beloved community. Lamenting together is what makes solidarity happen. We cultivate solidarity as we feel the weight of others' pain. In the process, beloved community grows, and a mutual longing for sustained change is born.

I believe that one reason why efforts toward racial reconciliation in the church stall is that we resist lament. This is understandable: Embracing lament means embracing pain! When it comes to racism, many of us prefer to *avoid* the pain or immediately jump in and *fix* the pain. Yet we can't enter into solidarity unless we're willing to suffer together with others.

In our wealth and comfort, many Christians today are more inclined to praise than to lament. Even though roughly 40 percent of the psalms are laments, a much tinier percentage of the songs that we sing at church today are laments. In fact, in a recent survey of the top one hundred worship songs, only five of the songs could qualify as a lament! Most of the songs reflect happier themes: "Glorious Day," "Happy Day," "Marvelous Light," "How Great Is Our God," and "Victory in Jesus."[4]

We can only dismantle racism to the extent that we are willing to bear racial pain in solidarity with suffering people.

Of course, nothing is wrong with praise songs! The problem is when we have an imbalance like we are experiencing now. There are no easy fixes to racism, no cut-and-paste solutions. We cannot praise our way through racism. We can only dismantle racism to the extent that we are willing to bear racial pain in solidarity with suffering people.

Earlier, I mentioned how Pastor Mark Vroegop engaged in sustained personal lament after the tragic passing of his stillborn daughter, Sylvia. This lament was key to his personal healing and reconnection with God. But there was more: God later prompted Mark to engage in racial reconciliation within his own congregation. As he did, he realized that just as lament had been key to his personal healing after the loss of his daughter, so also was lament key to the racial healing of his community. So he applied his learnings from personal lament to community lament, leading to his next book, *Weep with Me: How Lament Opens a Door for Racial Reconciliation*.[5] Vroegop's story is a beautiful example of how personal lament and group lament overlap and powerfully enrich one another. This is a game-changer for color-courageous disciples because it means that lament can empower us to be transformed as we transform the world.

There are many creative ways that communities can lament together in our pursuit of beloved community. We can more frequently voice prayers of lament in our worship services—not just after one-off racial tragedies, but as a regular part of our life together. We can buck the trend and regularly sing songs of lament. We can provide more education at church and at youth group about the grievous history of racism and its continuing impact on our world. We can share more stories of joy *and* pain. We can show up for one another while humbly promising to grow in our understanding.

In the end, lament may be the most powerful way to begin the journey toward beloved community, and lament may also be the most powerful way to sustain it.

THE GLORY OF DIVINE LAMENT

Effective color-courageous discipleship involves growing in our ability to process pain. Like you, I would rather not. If pain were an elective class, I would choose to skip it! Pain is disorienting. Pain is exhausting. Pain is no fun. Yet we know that as we lament through our pain, we can forge a deeper connection with God as well as deeper shalom in the world.

As we lament through our pain, we can forge a deeper connection with God as well as deeper shalom in the world.

But we're not done with lament yet. There is a third and even more mysterious type of lament that has the power to transform our pain—in fact, it is the most transformational kind. This third type of lament is *divine lament*—the lament of God himself. This is not lament that *we* do; it is lament that *God* does. Divine lament is lament that we *behold*. And in our beholding, we are transformed. Once we have eyes to see, we can find divine lament throughout the Scriptures—but we see divine lament most clearly in Jesus Christ.

Do you know where the word *excruciating* comes from? It's actually derived from the Latin word *crux*—meaning "cross"! Whenever I hear the word "excruciating," it reminds me that at the center of our faith, there is a God who bore upon himself the excruciating pain that was mine to bear. On the cross, Christ bore the harrowing pain of the whole world—thus defeating pain forever. And he did it in a posture of lament.

Although Psalm 22 is a psalm of David, we can understand it to be a psalm of Jesus too. That's because Jesus prayed the words of Psalm 22 on the cross, saying: "My God, my God, why have you forsaken me?" (Matthew 27:46). Jesus prayed this beautiful psalm of lament as some of his final words. Whenever I find myself feeling forsaken by God, do you know what I do? I envision Jesus there on the cross, speaking these words, suffering with me. When I begin to shed fresh tears in another moment of despair, I look up—and behold!—*I see a God there who is crying with me.* And you can too.

Like Christ, you can persevere through racial pain—and all pain that you experience—as you embrace God's gift of lament. Because Christ was forsaken in his pain, you never will be. As color-courageous disciples, we can behold the cross together and cherish the dazzling display of how God forever works through our pain to offer us possibility, purpose, and transformation.

THINK ABOUT IT

1. How do you feel about "praying in the raw"? Is it easy or hard for you to bring your real emotions to God? In what ways might you try this more often?

2. When in your life have you grown closer to God as a result of pain?

3. Lament can and should be considered a normal part of our prayer lives. What do you think about that statement? Why might it be helpful to consider lament a normal part of your prayer life?

4. What are some challenges that you are facing now? Where in your pain might there be opportunities to deepen your trust in God?

5. Why does the Bible call us to "weep with those who weep" (Romans 12:15, ESV)? Why do you think it might be especially helpful to weep or lament together with people of other races?

PILGRIMAGE (FOR PERSPECTIVE)

Pursue Transformation Through Incarnation

> Jesus *had* to go through Samaria because that's
> where the path of discipleship leads: right into the
> places where historic, systemic racial conflicts
> have led to division and strife.
>
> **—DAVID LEONG, *RACE AND PLACE***

Jars upon jars in a seemingly endless array, stretching from floor to ceiling—a kaleidoscope of earth colors in tan, clay, cocoa, and black. Standing here, I am startled and nauseated. Each jar brims with soil collected from the site of an American lynching. Each one represents priceless and unique lives, tragically lost. Each one echoes the ancient lament of our Lord: "What have you done? Listen! Your brother's blood cries out to me from the ground" (Genesis 4:10).

On this day, I am one in a group of pilgrims that has arrived at the Equal Justice Initiative in Montgomery, Alabama. This is a stop on the Sankofa Journey, a racial discipleship experience of the Evangelical Covenant Church. Before the journey, I had never heard of **Sankofa**, a word that is both beautiful and wise:

Lynching Jars, Equal Justice Initiative
PHOTO BY MICHELLE T. SANCHEZ

Sankofa is a word from the Akan tribe in Ghana. It means *San* (to return), *ko* (to go), *fa* (to fetch, seek, and take). The bird with its head turned backward taking an egg off its back embodies Sankofa's meaning. Sankofa attests that we must look backward (into our history), before we can faithfully move forward together, in the present and future. The Sankofa experience does just this, by exploring historic sites of the Civil Rights Movement, connecting the freedom struggle of the past to our present realities.[1]

Traditional Sankofa Bird

Our journey has included stops like the hotel where Martin Luther King, Jr., was murdered as well as the Edmund Pettus Bridge over which the "Bloody Sunday" protestors marched. More than ever before, I began to draw a bold, straight line connecting the past to the present—from slavery to lynching, to Jim Crow, to mass incarceration, and beyond.

BLOODY SUNDAY

On March 7, 1965, more than six hundred people marched across the Edmund Pettus Bridge in Selma, Alabama, to protest the suppression of African American voters. They were led by twenty-five-year-old activist John Lewis and joined by Martin Luther King, Jr. Although the Constitution now guarantees people of all races the right to vote, **voter suppression** still happens whenever some citizens make it harder for others to vote. Examples have included poll taxes, literacy tests, state laws, outright intimidation, and more. At the time of the march, African Americans in Dallas County, Alabama, comprised more than half of the population yet accounted for a mere 2 percent of registered voters.

ALABAMA DEPARTMENT OF ARCHIVES
AND HISTORY

On Bloody Sunday, state troopers violently attacked the peaceful voting rights demonstrators. Little did they know that their efforts would backfire: Widespread footage of the violence shocked the nation and galvanized new energy in the fight for racial justice.

To be honest, it was downright distressing. Looking back into the pain of the past is not fun. My grandparents purposely uprooted themselves from the South and relocated to the North—and, for the most part, they didn't look back. In a similar way, for much of my life, I had dealt with race by working to forget the past in order to move forward. Sometimes that can be helpful, of course. Even the Bible encourages us to "[forget] what is behind and [strain] toward what is ahead" (Philippians 3:13).

Yet the Scriptures *also* encourage us to proactively *remember* the past—for the sake of the present and the future. For example: "Remember the days of old; consider the generations long past. Ask your father and he will tell you, your elders, and they will explain to you" (Deuteronomy 32:7). Remembering is especially important when it comes to loving others well: "Continue to remember . . . those who are mistreated as if you yourselves were suffering" (Hebrews 13:3). Like most things in life, it is both/and—*the most fruitful way to move toward the future is with transformational wisdom gleaned from the past*. We must also draw near to the pain of both the past *and* the present if we hope to become a source of healing to others in the future. Given the contemporary landscape of our world—where racial pain is too often hidden or segregated away to specific places—drawing near to racial pain will often require a *literal* journey.

The most fruitful way to move toward the future is with transformational wisdom gleaned from the past.

Journeys like Sankofa are about not tourism but transformation. They engage travel not for the sake of play but for the sake of perspective. In the Evangelical Covenant Church, Sankofa has provided hundreds of disciples with a fully embodied opportunity to understand that racial righteousness is a critical component of discipleship in today's world. In this way, Sankofa has become a powerful expression of an ancient Christian spiritual practice called *pilgrimage*.

PILGRIMAGE AS A SPIRITUAL PRACTICE

A Christian **pilgrimage** is an intentional journey undertaken by disciples for the purpose of spiritual transformation. Although there are many types of pilgrimage, one characteristic common to them all is that they make you *move*. You can't be a pilgrim and a couch potato at the same time! The history of pilgrimage within the Christian church is long and rich:

> Although the words *pilgrim* and *pilgrimage* are absent from most English translations of the Bible, the image is a major one, encompassing some of the deepest meanings of what it means to be a follower and worshiper of God. . . . In both Testaments pilgrimage becomes a metaphor for the shape of the earthly life of anyone who is headed toward a heaven beyond this world.[2]

The Christian faith itself was born from a pilgrimage when God told Abraham, "Go from your country, your people and your father's household to the land I will show you"—and Abraham went. (Genesis 12:1). Now consider this: God could have worked in and through Abraham precisely where he was, right there in his hometown. All things are possible with God. But in his wisdom, God elected instead to work through pilgrimage. Later on, God sent Israel on a forty-year pilgrimage of purification in the wilderness. Echoing this, Jesus launched his ministry with a forty-day devotional pilgrimage in the desert. The theme of pilgrimage continues throughout the New Testament, in which the entire life of Christian discipleship is understood to be a pilgrimage.[3]

Pilgrims Leaving Canterbury, 1455–1462

For centuries, Christian disciples have imitated biblical models by embarking on their own pilgrimage journey as an intentional spiritual practice. Early Celtic *peregrini* set out "for the love of Christ" without having a particular destination.[4] Chaucer's fourteenth-century *Canterbury Tales* takes us on an adventure with a motley group that is holding a storytelling contest while on pilgrimage from London to a shrine in Canterbury. In the Middle Ages, countless pilgrims made their way to the Holy Land. Pilgrimage has long captured our imaginations. Did you know that, after the Bible, the most widely printed and translated book of all time is *The Pilgrim's Progress* by John Bunyan? As you might guess, it's a story about a religious pilgrimage!

Despite all this great history, though, here's the ironic thing: It is far more challenging for us to practice pilgrimage now— because now we take travel for granted! Planes, trains, and automobiles make traveling light-years easier than it was before.

Nevertheless, you can still engage in a meaningful pilgrimage today; you just need to be more intentional.

Why can pilgrimage still have a powerful impact on us? One reason is that pilgrimage engages our whole bodies. All teachers know that their students will learn faster and remember more when they use more of their five senses—sight, sound, smell, taste, and touch. And guess what? That's exactly what happens when you go on a pilgrimage.

But perhaps what is most powerful about pilgrimage is that it, simply by definition, spurs you to *move!* Today's church suffers from a bad case of "Couch Potato Christianity."[5] We are far too comfortable for our own good. It is no surprise then that our faith has become flabby and ineffective! Pilgrimage gets us moving again—challenging us to break through our comfort zones and recommit to the life of discipleship. Fair enough. But how can pilgrimage help us grow as color-courageous disciples?

THE PILGRIMAGE JESUS "HAD" TO TAKE

Of all the travel that Jesus did with the disciples, his journey to Samaria stands out. No other trip he took is described in this way: "So he left Judea and went back once more to Galilee. Now he had to go through Samaria" (John 4:3–4). *Had to?*

Strictly speaking, he didn't have to. Faithful Jews took the long way around Samaria. It would have been far easier to make a straight shot through Samaria. But faithful Jews knew that was a no-can-do.

Not so with Jesus. Befuddling his disciples again, Jesus made it clear that he was the kind of rabbi who went *through* Samaria— and he took his disciples with him. Why? Author David Leong tells us why in *Race and Place:* "Jesus had to go through Samaria because that's where the path of discipleship leads: right into the places where historic, systemic racial conflicts have led to divi-

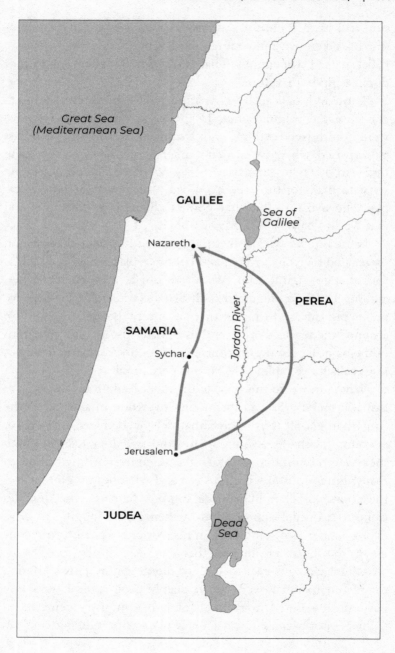

sion and strife."[6] Hmm . . . is that where your path of disciple-ship has taken you and your family? Right into places of systemic racial strife? I will confess: That's not typically where my path of discipleship has taken me!

Thousands of years later, we modern disciples aren't so differ-ent from the original ones. In the same way that the Twelve were flummoxed by the idea of a sojourn to Samaria, we're just as surprised when we are encouraged to visit—or even hang out!—in our own "Samarias" today. We especially do not know what to make of those pesky, social-justice-warrior-type disci-ples who make it sound like going to Samaria is still something that we all "have to" do. Says who?

Naturally, we still seek to "go around" places that remain segregated by race, poverty, and culture—places blighted by his-torical and systemic pain. We set up our homes, our churches, and our hearts in neighborhoods that are safe and strife-free; we prefer pilgrimage to places that are pretty. By default, we "go around" the places that remind us of hard history and inform us of the painful present. Of course we do—that's only natural. But Jesus calls his disciples to what is supernatural.

What's more, in this text, Jesus wasn't leading his disciples to Samaria merely (or even primarily) to swoop in and "save" the Samaritan people. Sure, the Samaritans needed a transformative encounter with Jesus—but so too did the disciples. Although they were committed to Jesus, the disciples remained blind to many dimensions of who Jesus was and what he was up to. Over the course of their pilgrimage through Samaria, the disciples came to a deeper appreciation of their Lord's longing to cross over boundaries of difference in his passionate pursuit to recon-cile us to God and to one another.

When we have eyes to see, we discover how Jesus's longing for reconciliation played out in deeply geographical ways. We have already noted how much of Jesus's ministry centered in Galilee—not because it was a lovely place with rolling green hills (which it was) but because it was known as Galilee "of the Gentiles," a thriving crossroads of Jewish and Gentile interaction.

But even after his sojourns in Samaria and Galilee, Jesus went further: "Then Jesus left Galilee and went north to the region of Tyre" (Mark 7:24, NLT). This was yet another surprising sojourn for a faithful rabbi: Tyre was a Gentile port city thirty miles north of Israel renowned for its worldliness. But it was in this place that Jesus had the opportunity to engage and bless the Syrophoenician woman, a descendant of *Canaanites,* no less—an even more ancient enemy of the Jewish people! It was a clear foretaste of the reconciliation to come for all—yes, even between God and Canaanites, even between Canaanites and Jews.

Throughout his life, Jesus crafted both discipleship and mission in specifically geographic ways: "Therefore go and make disciples of all nations" (Matthew 28:19). "And you will be my witnesses, telling people about me everywhere—in Jerusalem, throughout Judea, in Samaria, and to the ends of the earth" (Acts 1:8, NLT).

Clearly, today's disciples are not called to the exact same places as the original twelve disciples were. But that doesn't mean that geography doesn't matter for us at all. Discipleship has always had uniquely geographic dimensions; our task is to discern how those dimensions play out today.

RACE AND PLACE

We become more effective as color-courageous disciples when we learn to "think Christianly" about *place,* which means consistently asking not just *what* but *where.* Many of the most pressing racial crises that erupt in the news are deeply associated with place—concrete locations on the map, places we have already talked about in this book, like Flint, Michigan, or Ferguson, Missouri. As it turns out, place uniquely sheds light on race:

What place and geography do . . . is provide a window into the systems and structures of race so that we can see more clearly how racial issues . . . are not simply the result of "bad apples," or individual people with mean prejudices. Rather, the challenges of race that plague our cities are often rooted in how groups seek and maintain power (either implicitly or explicitly), how cultural patterns become physical structures, and how impersonal systems grow to protect the interests of those in power over time. In other words, geography reveals how race works systemically and not just individually.[7]

Did you know that the ethnic makeup of your neighborhood is not neutral? Historic practices like **redlining,** community resistance to low-income housing, and outright scare tactics—just to name a few—have consistently segregated Americans by race. The result is that while the United States has definitely become more diverse over time, for the most part, we are still living segregated lives. Most White people continue to live in majority-White neighborhoods, and most Black and Latino people live in majority non-White neighborhoods.[8]

---

*While the United States has definitely become
more diverse over time, for the most part,
we are still living segregated lives.*

REDLINING

Redlining is a historic discriminatory practice in the United States in which financial institutions denied people in certain neighborhoods loans and other services—usually, these were neighborhoods of color. The term *redlining* came about quite literally; banks would draw red lines around the neighborhoods that they deemed unworthy of investment. Although redlining is now illegal, it is important to understand that it has had long-lasting effects on our country. Redlining made it much harder for people of color to build wealth over time through homeownership. This is one major reason why African Americans today continue to have ten times less wealth than their White counterparts.

Most of us are so used to this segregated state of affairs that we rarely question it. Most probably don't think of it as a problem at all. After all, isn't it just proof that birds of a feather flock together? That is true to some extent, of course. But it masks the more foundational truth that the residential segregation we still experience today has not come about by the *personal preferences* of people of color. It has largely come about because of the *painful exclusion* of people of color over many years.

Why else is residential segregation not okay? Because, in reality, *separate still does not mean equal.* In fact, it's just the opposite. Too many communities of color have continued to experience severe systemic inequity. Why? Because "so many essentials to the American dream," such as quality schools, job opportunities, and retail and healthcare facilities, "are geographically constrained."[9]

Personally, I believe that one reason why many disciples remain unmoved by racial inequity is that they literally *do not see it.* The fact is that many of today's most grievous injustices of both race and class have been shuttled off to our modern-day Samarias. They are not only out of sight; they are out of mind—and heart.

Color-courageous disciples come to understand that society

remains segregated, and they seek to counteract this segregation. You may be wondering: *Is this whole conversation relevant to me? I didn't choose where I live now or where I go to school. I didn't make it hard for people to move to my neighborhood. I don't usually choose the places that I travel to.* All of that is, of course, true! At the same time, you have a special advantage because you still have your whole life ahead of you. You have not yet made many important "place" decisions—where to go to school, where to study abroad, where to do internships or mission trips, where to work, where to live. You have an advantage over adults who have already made many of those choices. Your life is just getting started. You have your whole future ahead of you to make a difference.

Now let's shift gears: In addition to remaining segregated *in space,* we also remain segregated figuratively *in time.* What I mean is that too many of us simply do not understand or appreciate the racial trauma that has happened in the past—the real pain that happened in real places and continues to impact those places today.

In the end, embarking on an antiracist pilgrimage experience is so powerful because it invites us to courageously protest our segregated lives and to literally reach across our divides in friendship and love.

PILGRIMAGE AS COLOR-COURAGEOUS DISCIPLESHIP

Before her first Sankofa journey, my friend Debbie Blue was apprehensive—not as much about the journey as about what it would unearth in her own heart. "I was afraid of the anger," she recalls. "I didn't want to go there."[10] But "go there" she did, and it transformed her life.

Debbie Blue facilitates racial discipleship for a bus full of
sojourners on a Sankofa pilgrimage

PHOTO BY SARAH SWANSON

For two decades, the Evangelical Covenant Church has conducted Sankofa pilgrimages for more than one thousand participants and counting. Over time, many have asked about the reasons that Covenant has flourished as a multiethnic evangelical denomination. The Sankofa pilgrimage is one of them. Although it is true that relatively few have taken the journey in comparison to our total Covenant population, it is also true that a fairly large proportion of Covenant *leaders* have experienced the journey. In this way, Sankofa has had an outsized impact on our church's unflagging commitment to multiethnic, antiracist ministry.

Originally pioneered by two Covenant leaders, one Black (Harold Spooner) and one White (Jim Lundeen), Sankofa was intended to provide our community with a truly immersive racial discipleship experience. The emphasis of Sankofa has been the exploration of the Black/White experience in America primarily because—with the important exception of Indigenous Americans—the Black/White story is the longest, and the inequities remain the widest. Our decision to begin with the Black experience in America has provided us a firm foundation on which to build a growing color-courageous engagement with all peoples, which is our ultimate goal.

At its heart, Sankofa is a Christ-centered journey that crosses divides and makes connections to real *places,* real *people,* and real *stories,* just as the disciples did on their pilgrimage to Samaria. A key component of the experience is that every person is assigned a partner for the journey, with at least one in every pair being a Black participant. The exact itinerary for each individual Sankofa journey has varied over time. Typically, the journey has started on a bus in Chicago followed by travels into the Deep South, making multiple stops at sites of major civil rights significance. Sankofa makes intentional connections between the *past* and the *present,* and therein lies its true transformational power: *Color-courageous disciples learn to discern the clear connecting lines between the racial inequities of the past and the racial inequities of the present.* If we can better understand those connecting lines, we may be better equipped to disrupt them.

Before taking my Sankofa journey, I had already heard someone give a lecture on mass incarceration at a conference—and that was valuable. However, learning in a classroom setting alone usually has a limited impact. Embodied experience makes all the difference—and that's what Sankofa was for me. After viewing those jars of lynching soil, we sat in a small auditorium where a tall, soft-spoken gentleman began to tell his story. Anthony Ray Hinton, who grew up poor and Black in Alabama, spent nearly thirty years on death row for a crime he did not commit. His story was a case study of the bias that is still embedded within our criminal justice system. The point was clear: Racial inequity in the criminal justice system is an ongoing reality that stretches from the past to the present. Suddenly, Hinton's story became part of my own. What was I going to do about it?

Reflecting on a similar realization from his own Sankofa journey, Jim Oberg, a White pilgrim from a Covenant church in

Owatonna, Minnesota, said that on Sankofa he came to realize that "Black history is everyone's history."[11] Now, whenever he encounters new stories of racial challenge, he says that he processes them differently: "Somehow they are now part of my story *because I have been there.*"[12] That is what pilgrimage does—it weaves our multicolored stories into a beautiful and complex tapestry that has the potential to produce real transformation of both oneself and the world.

They say that the shortest distance between people—and communities—is a story. If you go on a racial discipleship pilgrimage together with others, you can build bridges through storytelling. For example, as I mentioned earlier, participants on Sankofa are assigned a partner of a different racial background and given prompts to share their stories. Participants also hear additional stories through both films and live sharing. Individuals on pilgrimage can absorb stories through podcasts, magazines, audio tours, and live conversations with residents, tour guides, and museum staff.

> *The shortest distance between people—*
> *and communities—is a story.*

On pilgrimage, you also intentionally practice spiritual disciplines to actively engage God throughout the journey. Practices appropriate for a racial discipleship pilgrimage include lament, Scripture reading, prayer walks, fasting, feasting (eating together in diverse community), or ceremonies of remembrance. Almost any practice can catalyze discipleship when it is engaged with intentionality.

Pilgrimages like Sankofa also provide pilgrims of color with a dynamic way to process racial identity, pursue healing, and discern calling. As one younger Sankofa pilgrim of color reflects, "Dealing with my personal identity is why I went on this journey. . . . *You can read about things, but experiencing them in relationship with other people is far more life changing.*"[13] This pilgrim also says, "[Sankofa] served as a catalyst to what God has called me to be as a reconciler, a bridge builder."[14]

Back to my friend Debbie Blue: Even in the grip of her worries about what the experience would be like, she chose to courageously face her fears and embark on the journey. And guess what? As she faced her fears, they lost their power. In their place, she gained something new: confidence and passion for helping others to be reconciled and become reconcilers.[15]

Perhaps you will have the opportunity one day to go on a racial discipleship pilgrimage. Increasingly, these are being offered through schools, universities, denominations, and churches. Perhaps you can work with your youth pastor to create or join such a pilgrimage experience. I hope you will look out for (or help design!) such an opportunity. It could change your perspective forever.

FESTIVAL: PILGRIMAGE AT HOME

Here is a delightful truth: "Because the presence of God extends everywhere, even unto the very ends of the earth, pilgrimage can be practiced by anyone, anywhere, anytime."[16] Doing so, however, requires a shift in perspective:

> Pilgrimage, then, may refer to an inner—emotional, mental, and spiritual—journey as well as an outer, physical one: for Kempis [*The Imitation of Christ*] and Bunyan [*The Pilgrim's Progress*] it is possible for the pilgrim to remain in a cloister or a prison cell and yet go on a pilgrimage. Even so, inner pilgrimage, like its external counterpart, still implies *movement—toward a new spiritual state of being.*[17]

Let's now explore a biblical approach to doing "pilgrimage" at home: the seven Jewish festivals (or "feasts"). Of the seven, three are commonly referred to as "pilgrimage festivals" because they required all Israelite men to go on a physical pilgrimage to Jerusalem—Passover, Pentecost, and Tabernacles (Exodus 23:17; Deuteronomy 16:16). The psalms of ascent (Psalms 120–134) are a beautiful depiction of the heart of biblical pilgrimage, as they "were sung on pilgrim processions to Jerusalem and at the festivals that occurred there."[18] Although pilgrimage was required specifically for men, a pilgrimage was engaged whenever possible as an entire family or even an entire community. It is richly significant that the one story we have from Jesus's childhood takes place during a family Passover pilgrimage! (See Luke 2:41–52.)

For those who did not or could not go on pilgrimage—women, youth, the elderly, or anyone who was ill—God provided a creative solution: multisensory festivals. The biblical festivals, at heart, were fully immersive discipleship experiences designed to prompt remembrance, learning, and the forging of vital links between the past and the present. The Festival of Passover commemorates the deliverance of the Jews from slavery in Egypt. It is observed with a feast (*seder*), which symbolically tells the story through the elements of the meal. Bitter herbs represent the bitterness of bondage; lamb shank recalls the blood of the lamb shed for the Israelites' lives; and unleavened bread (*matzah*) recounts the swiftness of God's deliverance (see Exodus 12). During the weeklong Festival of Tabernacles, the Israelites constructed and resided in *sukkoth,* temporary shelters to remind them of God's provision through their forty-year sojourn in the wilderness.[19]

When pilgrimage is not possible, you can do a festival instead! The act of observing festivals with ethnic themes ideally serves a dual purpose. On the one hand, these festivals *foster multicultural appreciation.* We know that ethnicity is a God-ordained gift and that history will climax in a rich, multiethnic celebration—but why wait until then to enjoy the party? Festivals are meant to highlight the unique contributions, past and present, of each ethnic group. At the same time, festivals are also fantastic opportunities to intentionally *foster color-courageous awareness and action.* Racism has prevented us from enjoying all that every ethnic group has to contribute, both to the church and to the larger society. What has that looked like for each ethnic group—and what can we do about it now?

Here are some examples of what festivals have looked like for me. In the depths of the Covid-19 pandemic, when my family and so many others could not take a physical pilgrimage, we decided instead to celebrate the festival of **Kwanzaa** for the first time. Kwanzaa was established amid the Civil Rights Movement as a seven-day celebration of African American heritage. It was not originally a "Christian" holiday, but we infused it with Christian meaning. Since my husband is Colombian American, making my children Afro-Latino, we expanded it to include Latino heritage as well. Every day of Kwanzaa, we read a biography of a famous leader of color, reflected on all the challenges they overcame, and considered how we, too, could make a difference as color-courageous disciples of Christ. We ate traditional foods, lit symbolic candles, engaged in conversation, and enjoyed festive music. It was a blast!

Juneteenth, a festival that has been commemorated by African Americans for more than 150 years, celebrates the emancipation of enslaved people in the United States. Of course, there are also entire months designated to exploring communities of color (May for Asian American and Pacific Islander Heritage Month, September 15 through October 15 for National Hispanic American Heritage Month, etc.).

To be clear, all these festival experiences can be observed by anyone—in fact, that's the goal! They are not *just* for people of color. These festivals can be observed by both the designated group as well as their allies and friends. The whole point of something like Black History Month, after all, is to invite *everyone* to appreciate and benefit from Black cultures and contributions. And Christian churches, youth groups, and families can go one step further by creatively enriching them with faith-based meaning and color-courageous discipleship. The possibilities are endless.

RELOCATION: MAKING PILGRIMAGE PERMANENT

I would be remiss if I did not finish with this challenge: More of us should consider making pilgrimage long-term . . . or even permanent! John M. Perkins, civil rights luminary and founder of the Christian Community Development Association, has long identified pilgrimage as a powerful means of investing in a community: "How did Jesus love? . . . Jesus relocated. He became one of us. He didn't commute back and forth to heaven. . . . By relocating, a person will understand most clearly the real problems facing the poor. . . . Relocation transforms 'you, them, and theirs' to 'we, us, and ours.'"[20]

JOHN M. PERKINS

John M. Perkins (born June 16, 1930) is a Christian minister, civil rights leader, and community developer. He is co-founder of the Christian Community Development Association, an extensive network of Christians committed to seeing people and communities restored to shalom. After being raised in grinding poverty in the South, Perkins moved to California with his young family

John M. Perkins*
PHOTO BY PRISCILLA PERKINS

in search of a better life. As it turned out, Perkins didn't just meet some new neighbors in California; after he was invited to church there, he also met the author of life itself—Jesus Christ! Soon after, Perkins moved back home to Mississippi with a new mission to share the good news of Jesus Christ, starting with children and youth. Although Perkins's ministry initially emphasized *declaration* (sharing the gospel with words), he eventually expanded his ministry to holistically include *demonstration* (sharing the good news through deeds). Perkins is the author of several books, including *Dream with Me: Race, Love, and the Struggle We Must Win.*

* https://commons.wikimedia.org/wiki/File:JMP.jpg

In *The Power of Proximity,* Michelle Warren notes that "the most profound move you can make to address pain and injustice is to become proximate to it."[21] To become proximate means to get closer to something. Color-courageous disciples draw near despite their fears, and as they do, they discover not only *neighborhoods* but *neighbors.* My friend Dominique Gilliard encourages the church to "commission people to proximity." We need to

> get proximate to those people that the world has taught us to avoid. Those places and spaces that this world has taught us to do everything we can to actually go around. Those are the places I believe that we're actually called to be most intentional about going to, because when we go to those places, we actually get to see beyond the rhetoric, and we get to start to see that this is our brother and sister, this is our neighbor.[22]

As disciples seek to live out our most important mandate from Jesus to love our neighbor, more of us should at least consider *becoming* neighbors to those most in need. As a young person, you still have many possibilities in the years ahead to consider the different places where you might engage the world as a color-courageous disciple. What an incredible adventure!

Did you know that for Jesus, the word *neighbor* was most fundamentally an *action*? (For example, see Luke 10:36.) Jesus wants us to love others by being intentional about *how we neighbor.* So we would do well to routinely ask: "Jesus, where do you want me to live? Who do you want me to be a neighbor to, and why?" And remember: These are not once-and-for-all decisions! People now relocate multiple times in life. In fact, the average person now moves more than eleven times in their lifetime and holds ten different jobs before the age of forty! What might it look like for you to purposefully invest in an under-resourced community during one or more of your moves in life? If your eyes are open, you will be sure to discover numerous compelling opportunities.

While my husband and I currently live in a calm suburb of Chicago, for example, we have also lived in the teeming metropolis of New York City as well as an intentional community within a low-income Massachusetts neighborhood. We have lived in both apartments and houses. And twice, in order to serve the Lord in a particular place when we were more flexible, we lived in a basement with our kids! (To be clear, we now live above ground—but we still have some fond memories of those basements!) More recently, we have begun dreaming and discerning about if, when, and where God might have us relocate in the future for the highest kingdom impact.

When you are young, you are especially flexible when it comes to place. That's exciting—you have so many adventures open to you. I encourage you to look for opportunities for how God might work in and through you in a wide variety of places;

and be sure to seek the Lord about the place(s) where you will put down long-term roots. Regardless of where you are, if you are intentional, the Lord will make you blossom and bear fruit as a color-courageous disciple in the place where you are planted.

DISCIPLESHIP ISN'T A PICNIC—IT'S A PILGRIMAGE!

Billy Graham once joked that "Jesus invited us not to a picnic, but to a pilgrimage."[23] I hope that now you can understand why. Pilgrimage may be challenging, but precisely for this reason, it has the potential to transform us in outstanding ways.

The disciples were clueless as to why Jesus took them on a pilgrimage through Samaria. They were even more clueless—shocked speechless, actually—that Jesus chose to intentionally interact with a Samaritan woman there. Once she had departed, the disciples tried to avoid the embarrassing incident entirely by offering Jesus some lunch. He didn't fall for the distraction but said instead: "My food . . . is to do the will of him who sent me and to finish his work. Don't you have a saying, 'It's still four months until harvest'? I tell you, open your eyes and look at the fields! They are ripe for harvest" (John 4:34–35).

Due to our color-blind reading of the Scriptures, we usually think of these words as referring to evangelism—which they do! Yet when we read these words in living color, we understand that Jesus was referring to a more comprehensive vision of reconciliation with God *and* with one another. On pilgrimage, Jesus sought to open his disciples' eyes to the urgent work of *harvesting reconciliation*—both with God and across racial divides. As Leong urges us:

> I believe Jesus is calling his church again, just as he did with the disciples that day in Samaria, to open our eyes and look. The fields around us have been blighted by racial conflict and cul-

tural tensions, but they are ripe for reaping the fruit of reconciliation. By the Spirit, Jesus is continuing to move into our Samarias. I hope we will respond to Jesus' invitation to follow.[24]

The end of pilgrimage is actually not an end, but a start, "a gateway into a new way of being, of seeing life afresh with spiritually cleansed eyes."[25] Jesus took the disciples on pilgrimage to open not only the eyes of the *Samaritans* but also the eyes of the *disciples*—disciples like you and me. So let's get moving.

THINK ABOUT IT

1. How would you explain the symbol of the Sankofa bird to someone else? Why is it important for you to look back before you move forward?

2. In what ways is Christian discipleship more like a pilgrimage than a picnic?

3. We've learned that pilgrimage is an intentional journey undertaken by disciples for the purpose of spiritual transformation. Where would you be interested in going on racial pilgrimage, and why?

4. What festival(s) might you like to celebrate to better appreciate other cultures and racial experiences?

5. According to David Leong, "Discipleship leads us right into the places where historic, systemic racial conflicts have led to division and strife." Have you had such an experience before? Would you be open to this in the future? What might that look like?

FAST (FOR REAL)

Sacrifice Your Power to Build Beloved Community

> Fasting ... is not mere self-denial, but rather an earnest
> preparation for the feast of beloved community.
> —JONATHAN WILSON-HARTGROVE, *CHRISTIANITY TODAY*

So you might be thinking: *What in the world does fasting have to do with color-courageous discipleship?* I'm so glad you asked, because fasting is precisely where this whole book has been leading!

Okay, but now you're wondering, *Why? Is missing lunch really that important for antiracism?* The answer: nope. That's why I won't be talking too much here about missing lunch. What I *do* want to talk about is the disciple's call to self-sacrifice. **Fasting** is all about the spiritual practice of self-sacrifice. Traditionally, when we fast, we sacrifice the enjoyment of certain foods. But in reality, fasting has always pointed to something more profound: the denial of self in order to build beloved community.

Did you know that the Scriptures make a clear connection between fasting and justice? Listen to what God says about it: "Is not this *the kind of fasting I have chosen:* to loose the chains of injustice and untie the cords of the yoke, to set the oppressed free . . . and not to turn away from your own flesh and blood?" (Isaiah 58:6–7).

Fasting has always pointed to something more profound: the denial of self in order to build beloved community.

Since this kind of fasting is important to God, particularly when it comes to the formation of a just community, it should be important to us too. Because ultimately, fasting "is not mere self-denial, but rather an earnest preparation for the feast of beloved community."[1] In the end, color-courageous disciples will have maximum impact when they courageously choose to fast *for real*.

THE LORD'S CHOSEN FAST

There's no better place to learn about true fasting than the book of Isaiah. In Isaiah's time, people loved to show off their passion for God by engaging in lots of spiritual activities like making offerings, holding festivals, and getting together for assemblies. Ultimately, however, all their religious activities were not building beloved community. So, in God's eyes, all their religion was a massive exercise in missing the point!

Listen to God's own searing words about it in the very first chapter of Isaiah: "The multitude of your sacrifices—what are they to me? . . . Stop bringing meaningless offerings! . . . I cannot bear your worthless assemblies. . . . Your appointed festivals I hate with all my being. They have become a burden to me; *I am weary of bearing them*" (Isaiah 1:11, 13–14).

This is strong language. I think we can agree that worship that aggravates God is not quite what we're going for! So what kind of worship makes God smile? According to Isaiah 1:17, it is worship in which we "learn to do good; seek justice, correct oppression" (ESV). Let's look at this in more detail.

Learn (lāmad) *to do good:* the Hebrew word *lāmad* means to learn with the intention to put into practice. Here, it assumes that the people of God may not necessarily know how to do good. Though they follow God, they may remain blind to the ways that their actions perpetuate injustice. *Seek* (dāraš) *justice:* *dāraš* means to seek, inquire, or investigate. We don't just do cursory acts of charity and mercy—we level up by actively investigating ways to address problems at deeper levels. *Correct* (āšar) *oppression:* āšar means leading, guiding, setting right. As you participate in the restoration of the world, you multiply your impact as you guide others to do the same.

In sum: Isaiah teaches that spiritual practices that do not ultimately form us to do good, seek justice, and correct oppression in the real world become wearisome to God. Later, Isaiah 58 applies this to the spiritual practice of fasting. To this day, we continue to associate fasting with *serious* spirituality. Yet God was not pleased with their serious spirituality. "You cannot fast as you do today and expect your voice to be heard on high. Is this the kind of fast I have chosen, only a day for people to humble themselves? . . . Is that what you call a fast, a day acceptable to the LORD?" (Isaiah 58:4–5). Clearly not . . . something is still missing, and the Lord makes clear what that is:

> Is not this the kind of fasting I have chosen:
> > to loose the chains of injustice
> > and untie the cords of the yoke,
> to set the oppressed free
> > and break every yoke?
> Is it not to share your food with the hungry
> > and to provide the poor wanderer with shelter—
> when you see the naked, to clothe them,
> > and not to turn away from your own flesh and blood?
> Then your light will break forth like the dawn,
> > and your healing will quickly appear;

then your righteousness will go before you,
and the glory of the LORD will be your rear guard.
(Isaiah 58:6–8)

Why did God rebuke his people? Because their religion majored on navel-gazing—it was more about self-fulfillment than about fulfilling God's dream for beloved community. In the end, God desires that all our spiritual practices transform both us *and* our world. What does that look like when it comes to antiracism?

SACRIFICE YOUR POWER TO TRANSFORM YOUR WORLD

With the passing of years, I have increasingly realized that trying to change the world is usually folly. The list of people whose lives have measurably changed the entire world is quite short! Nevertheless, I can seek to change *my* world—my unique sphere of influence—on a daily basis. And you can seek to change yours. Don't worry about changing *the* world. Just seek to change *your* world.

This is precisely where fasting comes in. Just like God taught us in the book of Isaiah, today we can fast by choosing to make sacrifices to build beloved community. That's what we mean when we talk about fasting "for real." Rather than satisfying our own needs, fasting for real calls us to "satisfy the needs of the oppressed" (Isaiah 58:10). When we do, God promises to satisfy our own needs (58:11), working through us to rebuild the beloved community that was lost from the beginning. Listen to this beautiful promise: "Your people will rebuild the ancient ruins and will raise up the age-old foundations; you will be called Repairer of Broken Walls, Restorer of Streets with Dwellings" (58:12).

When it comes to antiracism, sacrificing power
may be the most important sacrifice that
color-courageous disciples can make.

Now hear this: When it comes to antiracism, sacrificing *power* may be the most important sacrifice we can make. And for that, Jesus is our perfect model: "Having loved his own who were in the world, he loved them to the end. . . . Jesus knew that the Father had put all things under his power . . . so he . . . began to wash his disciples' feet" (John 13:1, 3–5). Jesus calls us, as his disciples, to sacrifice power for love too (John 13:12–17).

Power Audit Practice

I get it: Most disciples do not think of themselves as "power-ful." I'm guessing that *most* of us don't go around thinking about how powerful we are! Especially if you're young. So let's reframe power in a way that we can relate to. The truth is that we *all* enjoy different types of power to different degrees within our spheres of influence—regardless of our ages or stages in life. And we can learn to leverage those powers for good.

Friend, if there is only one next step that you take from reading this book, please make it a **power audit**—the ongoing practice of identifying the power you hold and discerning what to do with that power. When someone does an *audit,* it means that they do a very careful review. So, when you take a power audit, it means that you carefully review your life and consider the types of power you have in different dimensions of your life.

Let's consider four types of power that are vital for color-courageous disciples: (1) **privilege,** (2) **position,** (3) **platform,** and (4) **prosperity.** As you can see, I've arranged these four types of power into the shape of a cross. That's because I pursue these sacrifices of power as a means of taking up my cross daily in love (Luke 9:23). The first step of the power audit practice is to identify what each of these four types of power looks like in your own life at any given time or in any given place. The second step is to discern tangible ways that you can leverage or sacrifice your power in each of the four areas for the sake of building beloved community. For a free handout that you can use for the power audit practice, please visit https://michelletsanchez.com/color courageous.

The power audit practice will be even more transformational and effective if you take a third step and share it with other color-courageous disciples who can provide accountability and encouragement as you continue the journey. Consider the very word *encouragement*—to give courage. We were never meant to pursue the color-courageous discipleship journey alone. We were meant to encourage one another, giving one another courage in the work of building communities of love (Hebrews 10:25).

Although we may not find the phrase *power audit* in the Bible, I believe that we see it at work in the life of Queen Esther as she identifies her power and then makes sacrifice after sacrifice. She is, for me, a stunning portrayal of what it means to be color-courageous. Let's turn to her story now.

INTRODUCING ESTHER, THE
COLOR-COURAGEOUS QUEEN

As the story opens, we meet a marginalized community of Jewish people living as an ethnic minority group in Persia. King Xerxes and his wife, Vashti, have a major falling out—so he kicks her to the curb. He wants a new queen, but unfortunately, there were no dating apps in those days! So instead, the king decides to launch a beauty pageant. Esther, a young Jewish orphan, sees this as her Cinderella moment: She hides her ethnic identity, wins the pageant, and is ushered into royalty. Exciting, right?

Well, unfortunately, Esther's story doesn't end here with a "happily ever after." Haman, the king's right-hand man, despises the Jews and convinces the king to slaughter them all on a specific date. How does Esther respond? *By fasting—not just from food but,* *more importantly, from power.* At the

Queen Esther, Edwin Long, 1878

possible cost of her own life, Esther finally reveals her ethnic identity to the king and successfully pleads for the lives of her people. In a stunning reversal, *Haman* is put to death, and the entire Jewish community is saved! To this day, Jews celebrate this stunning turn of events through a festival called Purim (Esther 9).

Now here's a curious thing: Did you know that fasting is the *only* spiritual practice named in the whole book of Esther? Not even worship or prayer are mentioned—or clearly practiced—anywhere in the book. That makes me wonder: *Perhaps that's because we are meant to pay special attention in the book of Esther to fasting—fasting for real.* I think it's critical that we don't miss this! In this story, Esther fasts from food—yes. But far more importantly, she fasts from *power.* She willingly sacrifices privilege, position, platform, and prosperity to love her community. Let's take a closer look at each.

1. Privilege: How are you utilizing your unearned advantages for good?

When we talk about privilege, we're simply referring to an unearned advantage. There are many types of privilege, but we are focusing on racial privilege. In most societies, there is an invisible social hierarchy in which some races, ethnicities, or cultures have greater status than others—and greater status means more advantages. We can call these advantages **racial privilege.**

Let's take America, for example, where "Whiteness" has historically been bestowed with advantage. There is, of course, nothing *inherently* beneficial about being born as a White person. Still, "White" has been equated in our country with "normal" and "better" for hundreds of years. For example, as we learned from the research in chapters 3 and 4, White people are less likely to be harshly disciplined at school or pulled over in their cars. They are also more likely to receive a job interview or to be approved for a mortgage so that they can buy a home. These are all examples of unearned advantages. Of course, I do understand that not all White people *feel* advantaged or somehow magically experience everything to be easier in life. In fact, plenty of White people find themselves worse off than many people of color—and for that matter, many other White people! That's why it also helps me to understand privilege as *the absence of certain disadvantages.* I like how David Swanson, a White pastor and a friend of mine, puts it: "This is not to say that White people in America do not face injustices, even systemic ones— only that we don't face them *because of our race.*"[2]

With all that being said, let's understand: Privilege is not something that only White people have. Unearned advantage comes in countless varieties. We see this in Esther's story. Esther did not have privilege because of her ethnicity. Her ethnicity was a clear disadvantage. However, Esther *was* privileged with stunning beauty, which was a "privilege" in that she did nothing to earn or deserve it. Nevertheless, she still had the responsibility to decide *how* she would utilize her God-given privilege of beauty, whether for selfish purposes or for some greater purpose.

I can relate to Esther. As a Black woman, I have always thought of myself as disadvantaged. And in many ways, that is true. At the same time, I've come to understand that I *also* have been given many advantages. Yes, I have privilege too—and lots of it. For example, I did nothing to be born into a middle-class family and raised in a neighborhood with well-resourced schools. Nevertheless, these realities have given me advantages in life that others have not enjoyed. So I also have the responsibility of answering the question: How can I use my unearned advantages for good?

The concept of **intersectionality** can help us identify and leverage the unique advantages and disadvantages we may hold due to overlapping identities in different, ever-shifting contexts. It prompts us to ask the questions: *In my current context, what are my disadvantages and what are my advantages? And what will I do with these?* When we view Esther's story through the lens of intersectionality, we can identify her *disadvantages* as being a woman and a marginalized ethnic minority. Yet we can also identify her *ad-*

vantage of stunning beauty, which allowed her to access the most powerful people and resources in the land. And get this: Esther's growing awareness of both her disadvantages *and* her advantages are key to her becoming a hero in this story. Ultimately, we still read about Esther today because she chose to sacrificially leverage her privileged beauty for the sake of her community.

> ***Esther's growing awareness of both her disadvantages** and **her advantages** are key to her becoming a hero in this story.*

Of course, Jesus did exactly the same with his own "privilege." Jesus came into the world with the status of equality with God, yet Jesus "did not consider equality with God something to be used to *his own advantage*" (Philippians 2:6). Isn't that amazing? Instead, he lovingly sacrificed his personal advantage to save our lives and make us whole.

2. Position: How can you utilize for good the positions you hold?

Position is about your roles as well as the spheres of influence that come with those roles. These include both *relational roles* (brother, friend, daughter) as well as *organizational roles* (youth group leader, sports team captain, student government secretary). The power of position can be outright and obvious. Perhaps more often, though, the power that comes with position is quiet and unseen. Do you remember how Hamilton put it in the musical? At the end of the day, power comes down to being "in the room where it happens"![3] *Position* is what grants you access to the room where it happens. In a family, that room may be the dining room; in a school, the classroom; in a company, the boardroom.

Back to Esther's story: The real climax is the moment Esther realized that she had to make a choice. What would she do with her position? She had to consider: *Will I use my position to save my own life? Or will I use it to save my people . . . and potentially lose my position as a consequence?*

Notice that Esther ultimately processed these questions not by herself, but in community, with her cousin Mordecai. Mordecai encouraged Esther—that is, he prompted her to have courage. Despite the risk, he challenges Esther to intervene: "Who knows but that you have come to your royal *position* for such a time as this?" (Esther 4:14). I love this question for so many reasons. Most of all, I love it simply because it is a *question*. Mordecai prompted Esther to wonder about a question that all color-courageous disciples should consider: *How might God be inviting you to leverage whatever position you have for his glory?* After all, that is precisely why God has gifted you with position in the first place.

As a color-courageous disciple, you can *leverage* the positions you hold throughout life to make a difference. A student body president can consider ways to make sure students of color are included, and a youth group leader can suggest that the group try a color-courageous discipleship pilgrimage. Parents can engage their families in color-courageous discipleship, and Sunday school teachers can include racial discipleship in the curriculum.

As you continue the journey from here, remember this: Many of the positions that you will hold in life will be temporary—so time is of the essence! You have God-given opportunities *right now* to dismantle racism—opportunities that will not last forever. What would it look like for you to make the most of your positions for such a time as this?

WHAT MAKES THE BOOK OF ESTHER UNIQUE?

- Esther is one of only two books in the Bible *named after a woman*. (The other one is Ruth.)
- Esther is the only book of the Bible where *God is not named*. Yet God is clearly at work in her story!
- The only spiritual discipline specifically mentioned in the book of Esther is *fasting*.
- Jewish people still celebrate Esther's courageous actions to save her people every year on *a holiday called Purim*.

3. Platform: How can you stand up and speak out for good?

While the power of position is often exercised quietly, platform is about taking a public stand. It is about courageously *standing up* and *speaking out* for what is right on someone else's behalf. Anyone who has a voice has a platform, and you can leverage that platform by publicly advocating for antiracism. In the Bible, we learn that **advocacy** is a vital practice for the people of God: "Defend the weak and the fatherless; uphold the cause of the poor and the oppressed" (Psalm 82:3).

Advocacy is a vital part of building beloved community: "We reflect God's love when we call on leaders to protect the most vulnerable. . . . Providing direct assistance to people in need is vital, but it is also important to . . . partner with marginalized communities for long-term change, and to *speak up for policies that empower all people*."[4]

"Speak up for those who cannot speak for themselves."

Note that advocacy often comes down to engaging *policies*. A **policy** is simply a high-level plan—all countries, organizations, and communities need policies to function. And what we have learned is that, unfortunately, systemic racism persists through policies that continue to produce racial inequity—whether intentionally or unintentionally. Esther was color-courageous in that she utilized her platform to oppose an unjust ethnic policy. The Jewish people were suddenly confronted with an unjust *policy* of ethnic genocide—and they certainly did not have the power to speak for themselves. But Esther *did* have the God-given power of voice. So, Mordecai implored her not to "remain silent" but to use her voice in advocacy (Esther 4:14).

Anyone who approached the king unbidden faced a potential death sentence. Nevertheless, Esther made her choice: "Go, gather together all the Jews who are in Susa, and fast for me. . . . I and my attendants will fast as you do. When this is done, I will go to the king, even though it is against the law. *And if I perish, I perish*" (Esther 4:16).

I love how the Latin word *vox* ("voice") and the word *vocare* ("to call") are related. Whenever you are called (*vocare*) to be courageous, it will typically involve raising your voice (*vox*) in some way. Doing so comes with consequences—both positive and negative. Nevertheless, color-courageous disciples are called to the risk of raising their voice. Will there be pushback? For sure. This is what Jemar Tisby says about pushback in *How to Fight Racism*:

> There will be those who question why "you're making this about race." Others will want to argue endlessly about a particular turn of phrase or one part of your actions rather than attending to the general thrust of what you're trying to say. Some will disavow you. . . . But you should be prepared for positive reactions too. . . . No matter what the reaction or the ratio of positive to negative responses, using your platform to promote racial justice is simply the right thing to do.[5]

Leveraging our platform to build beloved community is simply the right thing to do. What's more, due to social media, YouTube, and a myriad of ever-growing online opportunities to address the world, I believe that younger generations now have access to a platform that is greater than anything previous generations have had. How will you use yours?

4. Prosperity: How can you give more generously of your time, talent, and treasure to foster biblical equity?

As color-courageous disciples, we are invited to give generously in order to build beloved community—with an emphasis on advancing equity. Prosperity takes many forms, so it helps to identify the resources we may have at our disposal through the oft-referenced trio of time, talent (skills, education), and treasure (finances, possessions). Throughout life, you will enjoy different levels of prosperity in each category. As a young person, you are rich in time; creatives are rich in skills and ideas; professionals may be rich in financial resources.

Color-courageous disciples of all ages can find ways to practice everyday generosity when it comes to their time, talent, and treasure. For example:

- *Time: Where can you or your community devote regular time to antiracism?* Our time is the most valuable resource we have because it is the most limited! Plus, nothing else can happen without the investment of time. You can use your time to continue growing in awareness (or help others to do so), to cultivate relationships, or to volunteer where needed.
- *Talent: What specialized skills could you or your community offer to advance antiracism?* Many minority-led or antiracist-focused ministries and nonprofit organizations are under-

resourced in many ways. Consider: What skills do you have that may be of value to others, including knowledge of graphic design, technology, social media, food preparation, and beyond?

- *Treasure: Where can you or your community steward your finances to support antiracism?* Think about this both individually and corporately. How does your church or youth group financially partner with minority-led organizations through financial support? Instead of asking adults in your life for one more Christmas gift, how about you ask them to make a donation in your name? Where can you personally give to make a difference? Remember the story of the widow's offering: Even small offerings can make a big difference (Luke 21:1–4).

Was Esther prosperous? Yes and no. Despite her royal status, Esther was fully dependent on others. In other words, she did not have her own bank account to manage as she wished. Nevertheless, she figured out how to access the resources that she *did* have access to simply because she was queen. Through a series of lavish banquets that she requested and hosted, she accessed the prosperity available to her in order to engage in effective advocacy.

THE COURAGEOUS EMBRACE OF THE CROSS

And so we discover where the journey of color-courageous discipleship—like *all* discipleship—has been leading us: to the courageous embrace of the cross. We usually associate courage with valiant feats. But the kingdom of God has always been an upside-down kingdom in that things are often the opposite of what you expect. Jesus demonstrated with his own life that it is more courageous to rely on God than to defy God; to turn the other cheek rather than lash out; to serve rather than be served;

to share rather than hoard; to sacrifice oneself rather than fixate on oneself. All of this requires us to take the courageous risk of trusting God with our lives.

Will you experience hardship, loss, or pain in your pursuit of color-courageous discipleship? Yes—that's pretty much guaranteed. Why else would you need courage? Yet remember this: Every cross is temporary, and on the other side of the cross, there is joy and new life that can be found no other way. Thankfully, Jesus has gone before us: "For the joy set before him he endured the cross, scorning its shame, and sat down at the right hand of the throne of God. . . . Consider him . . . so that you will not grow weary and lose heart" (Hebrews 12:2–3). Recall that "heart" is at the core of what courage is all about. We will survive and thrive as color-courageous disciples as we focus on Jesus Christ. And as we focus on him, we will become more like him. We will experience the surprising presence of Jesus at work in and through us to transform our world. I love how C. S. Lewis described this Christ-transformation: "Every Christian is to become a little Christ. The whole purpose of becoming a Christian is simply nothing else."[6]

Esther has been for us a beautiful foreshadowing of what a "little Christ" looks like. Have you ever heard of a *Christ figure*? A Christ figure is a character in a story whose life is modeled after Jesus Christ's in some way—usually, in sacrificing oneself to save someone else. People typically think of Christ figures as male. But I would make the case that Esther is one of the most extraordinary Christ figures in all Scripture! Esther sacrificed her God-given privilege, position, platform, and prosperity—and was even willing to sacrifice her life—for others. In the process, she saved her entire community! Truly, Esther is one of my all-time heroes. There were many forms of power that Esther did not have. But her story is a brilliant illustration of what it looks like to identify the power that one *does* have and sacrificially use it for good. It is simply breathtaking.

Like Esther, we, too, can take color-courageous action in God's power. And, like Esther, we may also experience the promise of Isaiah 58: "If you do away with the yoke of oppression . . . then your light will rise in the darkness" (verses 9–10). And as God's light shines through us in the darkness, people will see it and rejoice. Color-courageous disciples have the beautiful potential not only to build beloved community but also to save lives as we see new disciples made in the process!

Now, of course, we have an even more brilliant model than Esther: Jesus Christ our Savior, who not only inspires us but also empowers us through his Spirit. This reminds me of the occasion in the Scriptures where eager crowds surrounded Jesus and asked: "What must we do to do the works God requires?" (John 6:28). That is, more or less, the question we've been asking: *When it comes to racism, what is the work that God requires?* Jesus's answer to us now is the same as it was then: "The work of God is this: to believe in the one he has sent" (verse 29). There is a Savior—and, thankfully, it's not us.

Jesus launched his ministry with a forty-day sacrifice of food. He concluded his ministry by sacrificing his reputation, his communion with his Father, and his very life. In sacrificing not only his *power* but *life itself,* Jesus made the way for us to enjoy God's beloved community forever. Now, Jesus invites color-courageous disciples to become "little Christs" and follow in his steps: "I have set you an example that you should do as I have done for you" (John 13:15).

May God bless you from here and make his face to shine upon you, now and always, as you pursue new adventures on the color-courageous discipleship journey!

THINK ABOUT IT

1. At its heart, fasting isn't about food but sacrifice. In your own words, how would you describe what it means to fast "for real," and why does God prefer this type of fasting from his disciples?

2. What do you find most inspiring or interesting about Esther's story?

3. Use the power audit cross to consider this: How might you sacrifice your power to love others as a color-courageous disciple now or in the future? (You can download a power audit cross worksheet at http://michelletsanchez.com/colorcourageous.) Be specific about what leveraging or sacrificing your privilege, position, platform, and prosperity might look like.

4. What have been one or two of the greatest takeaways of the color-courageous discipleship journey for you?

5. Where would you like your color-courageous discipleship journey to take you from here?

GLOSSARY

AAPI. Asian American and Pacific Islander.

Advocacy. The practice of standing up and speaking out, typically on someone else's behalf, for what is right. (Chapter 10)

Agape Love. The self-giving, sacrificial, supernatural love of God that casts out all fear. Beloved community is characterized by agape love between people of all ethnicities. (Chapter 6)

Ambassadors of Reconciliation. All disciples have been appointed by God to be agents of God's reconciliation to the world (2 Corinthians 5:11–21). Disciples have the power to be agents of reconciliation on every level of creation—personal, corporate, systemic, and cosmic. (Chapter 2)

Antiracism. The practice of becoming aware of and uprooting personal racial prejudice plus working to dismantle systemic practices that lead to racial inequity. The shorthand for antiracism is Uprooting Personal Prejudice + Dismantling Systemic Inequity. (Chapter 1)

Assimilation. The downplaying of one's ethnic distinctiveness in order to better fit in with the dominant group. (Chapter 5)

Attribution Error. A cognitive bias that causes people to attribute blame in lopsided ways. *Ultimate attribution error,* for example, causes us to blame a community or people group for their plight rather than adequately taking situational factors into account. (Chapter 4)

Beloved Community. A phrase popularized by Martin Luther King, Jr., to describe a loving, diverse society. A community grounded in Christlike, agape love for God and for one another amid all our differences. It is also characterized by solidarity, interdependence, and biblical equity. (Chapters 1 and 6)

Bias Blind Spot (see **Truth Distortion**). The tendency of people to believe that they are less biased than other people. (Chapter 4)

BIPOC. Black, Indigenous, and People of Color. This term draws attention to the fact that Black and Indigenous people historically have been at a greater systemic disadvantage in North America than other people of color.

Black. Generally refers to people of African descent.

Black Lives Matter. A decentralized movement comprised of people of all racial backgrounds that is dedicated to raising awareness and inspiring change regarding the racial inequity experienced by Black people. (Chapter 3)

Blame (category **Unconscious Bias**). The human inclination to blame a person's behavior on their character rather than on their circumstances or any other mitigating factors. (Chapter 4)

Brown. An overarching term that refers to people of color with "brown" skin who are not Black, including people of Latino/a, Indigenous, Middle Eastern, or South Asian descent.

Chinese Exclusion Act. A nineteenth-century federal law that prohibited the immigration of Chinese people to the United States. (Chapter 4)

Cognitive Bias. A misperception of the mind; an unconscious bias. (Chapter 4)

Colonialism. The act of powerful countries exerting control over other countries. European colonialists needed a simple excuse to demean people and steal their land. So, they created this thing called "race" as a solution. (Chapter 1)

Color blindness. The belief that racism can be overcome by "not seeing" color and treating everyone the same. Unfortunately, those who cannot "see" color also tend to overlook racial disparity. (Chapter 4)

Color-Courageous. The opposite of color blindness; those who are color-courageous choose to "see color" (race and ethnicity) for the sake of cultivating racial equity. (Chapter 4)

Color-Courageous Discipleship. The courageous, lifelong journey of following Jesus, dismantling racism, and building beloved community. (Chapter 1)

Colorism. The prejudice that assigns higher value and beauty to lighter skin tones. (Chapter 5)

Community Cultural Wealth. The uniquely rich contributions that each culture can make to the world; includes knowledge, values, skills, artifacts, wisdom accumulated from common experiences, and more. (Chapter 7)

Confirmation Bias (see **Truth Distortion**). The tendency to see what we want to believe, even if it's false. (Chapter 4)

Crabs-in-a-Bucket Effect. One crab in a bucket can escape without a problem. But a group of crabs in a bucket will drag down individual ones that try to escape, irrationally ensuring the demise of the whole group. Similar dynamics have been observed in marginalized communities. (Chapter 5)

Criminalization (category **Unconscious Bias**). A category of unconscious bias in which certain ethnic groups are seen to be more dangerous, guilty, or worthy of punishment. (Chapter 4)

Cruciform. Taking the shape of a cross. Like all disciples, color-courageous disciples are called to cruciform love for the sake of building beloved community. (Chapter 6)

Decentering. Moving from believing that one's own culture is central to understanding that one's cultural perspective is one among many in a rich tapestry of unique cultural perspectives. (Chapter 7)

Defensive Othering. The practice of distancing oneself from one's own racial or cultural group. (Chapter 5)

Dehumanization (category **Unconscious Bias**). Humans tend to assume that those who are not like us share our humanity to a lesser degree. When a person or group is considered to be less than human, it becomes easier to mistreat them. (Chapter 4)

Disciple (or **Discipleship**). Jesus made this invitation to his first disciples: "Follow Me, and I will make you fishers of people" (Matthew 4:19, NASB). A disciple (1) follows Jesus, (2) is transformed by Jesus, and (3) is on mission with Jesus. (Chapter 1)

Discrimination (or **Racial Discrimination**). The act of treating people from different racial groups differently, resulting in some racial groups receiving worse treatment than others. (Chapter 1)

Divine Racial Trauma. Racial trauma that has a negative impact on one's relationship with God. (Chapter 5)

Environmental Racism. A form of racial inequity in which communities of color are disproportionately exposed to pollutants or denied the high-quality municipal services that others enjoy. (Chapter 5)

Epigenetics. A field of scientific inquiry that studies heritable changes in gene expression, such as those observed in transgenerational racial trauma. (Chapter 5)

Equality. Equality emphasizes sameness; for example, we are all equal in that we all possess the same image of God. In conversations about race, those who emphasize equality tend to advocate for people to be treated the same regardless of whether or not their starting points are equal (contrast with **Equity**). (Chapters 3 and 6)

Equity (or **Biblical Equity**). Equity emphasizes fairness. The goal of biblical equity is not to force particular outcomes but to provide everyone with fair opportunities to exercise their God-given gifts. In conversations about race, those who emphasize equity typically acknowledge that people have different starting points; they therefore seek a customized approach to achieve fair opportunity (contrast with **Equality**). (Chapters 3 and 6)

Ethnicity. A God-ordained cultural identity that God delights in as a means of bringing glory to himself and enrichment to his kingdom. (Chapter 1)

Ethnocentrism. The belief that one's ethnic group is normative and/or superior to others. (Chapter 1)

Evangelical. Christians of all ethnic backgrounds who take the Bible seriously and believe in Jesus Christ as Savior and Lord. (Chapters 6 and 7)

Fasting. Abstaining from food or drink for a purpose. A Christian approach to fasting also entails abstaining from other resources, including forms of power like **Privilege, Position, Platform,** or **Prosperity** for the sake of achieving biblical equity and building beloved community. (Chapter 10)

Gospel. The gospel is the good news that Jesus Christ is Lord and Savior; through his crucifixion and resurrection, Jesus has provided the free gift of salvation to sinners and is reconciling all creation to himself. (Chapter 2)

Hate Crime. A crime, typically involving violence, that is committed on the basis of prejudice. In recent years, hate crime in America has risen to levels not seen in a decade. (Chapter 5)

Historical Racial Trauma. The emotional and psychological injury that collectively impacts a person's entire lifespan and entire communities. It can include mental illness, family dysfunction, alcohol abuse, and even premature mortality and has been observed among Black communities (dubbed "post-traumatic slave syndrome"), Japanese Americans (after the internment camps of World War II), and Jewish communities (after the Holocaust). (Chapter 5)

Image of God (*Imago Dei*). *Imago dei* is a Latin term meaning "image of God." Color-courageous disciples recognize that all people are equally created in God's royal image, and as such, we should seek to treat everyone with dignity and resist dehumanization of all kinds. (Chapter 5)

Implicit Bias. Another name for **Unconscious Bias.** (Chapter 4)

Individualism. A cultural lens that understands the individual, rather than the collective, to be paramount. (Chapter 7)

Intention vs. Impact Dilemma. Names the reality that our intentions do not always have the impact that we desire. For example, while a person might *intend* to treat people of all races equally, unconscious bias may still cause the person to negatively *impact* others through unequal treatment. (Chapters 4 and 7)

Intercultural. Intentional engagement between cultures that results in mutual insight and transformation. (Chapter 7)

Interdependence. The state of being dependent on one another, as are members of the body of Christ. Regardless of our placement in the body of Christ, we are inescapably connected and need the rich and surprising gifts that God grants in and through one another. (Chapter 6)

Internalized Racism (also, **Internalized Oppression**). Racism that is not external but internal; internalized racism happens when a marginalized racial group internalizes society's negative narratives about themselves. (Chapter 5)

Intersectionality. A framework for understanding the dynamics of overlapping identities in whatever context we might find ourselves. (Chapter 10)

Juneteenth. A U.S. holiday observed on June 19 that celebrates the emancipation of slaves in the United States. Juneteenth does not commemorate the date that Abraham Lincoln issued the Emancipation Proclamation (September 22, 1862); rather, Juneteenth commemorates the date that slaves in Texas were finally liberated by the Union army upon the close of the Civil War (June 19, 1865). Juneteenth has been celebrated by many African Americans in the United States for over 150 years. In 2021, Juneteenth was declared a U.S. federal holiday. (Chapter 9)

Kingdom of God. An all-encompassing term for the rule of Jesus Christ on earth; includes every dimension of creation. (Chapter 6)

Kwanzaa. A seven-day celebration of African American heritage that is observed from December 26 to January 1. The term *Kwanzaa* is Swahili for "harvest." (Chapter 9)

Lament. A prayer of pain that leads to trust; its four key steps are turn, complain, ask, and trust. (Chapter 8)

Magis. A Latin word that means "more" or "greater." The Ignatians (Society of Jesus) have used the concept of *magis* as a reminder that Jesus continually invites his disciples to more. Color-courageous disciples seek to abide in Christ more deeply so that they might bear Christ's fruit more abundantly. (Chapter 3)

Majority. A synonym for **White** people. The term is waning in usage because the United States is soon projected to have a majority of **People of Color.** (Chapter 1)

Mass Incarceration. Mass incarceration is the disproportionate incarceration of a group of people relative to the general population. (Chapter 3)

Meritocracy. A system which, when functioning rightly, rewards everyone on the basis of merit and skill. (Chapter 6)

Minority. A synonym for **People of Color.** The term is waning in usage because the United States is soon projected to be minority White. (Chapter 1)

Noetic Effect of Sin. *Noetic* means "relating to mental activity or the intellect." The noetic effect of sin means that sin has compromised the human ability to process information, discern truth, and perceive the world accurately. One example of this in race relations is **Unconscious Bias.** (Chapters 2 and 4)

Ostrich Effect (see **Truth Distortion**). The tendency to avoid unpleasant information, even if it's true. (Chapter 4)

Pentecost. The church's colorful birthday. On Pentecost, God poured out his Holy Spirit on the disciples as diverse tongues of fire, clearly demonstrating his intention for the church to embrace people from every tribe, tongue, people, and nation. (Chapters 1 and 6)

People of Color (POC). An overarching term for non-White people that typically includes African Americans, Native Americans, Asian Americans, Latino Americans, and Arab Americans. (Chapter 1)

Perpetrator Trauma or **Perpetration-Induced Traumatic Stress (PITS).** A form of PTSD (post-traumatic stress syndrome) that emerges after a person traumatizes someone else. (Chapter 5)

Pilgrimage. A journey taken for the purpose of spiritual transformation. (Chapter 9)

Platform (category **Power Audit**). Platform is about utilizing one's voice and taking a public stand; it is also about elevating other voices that deserve to be heard. (Chapter 10)

Policy. A high-level plan. All organizations and communities need policies to function. Unfortunately, systemic racism tends to persist through policies that continue to produce racial inequity, whether intentionally or unintentionally. (Chapter 10)

Position (category **Power Audit**). A role, typically one that also bestows a sphere of influence. We have access to spheres of influence through our *relational roles* (brother, friend, daughter) as well as *organizational roles* (youth group leader, sports team captain, student government secretary). (Chapter 10)

Post-Traumatic Growth. The positive transformation that can be experienced as a result of the struggle with a traumatic event. (Chapter 5)

Power Audit. The practice of identifying the different types of power that one has and considering ways to leverage those powers to do good. (Chapter 10)

Powers and Principalities. The Scriptures reveal that there are larger forces of evil at war against God; these include deceptive and destructive human ideologies like racism. Disciples are called to identify and prayerfully resist the powers and principalities of the world in God's power. (Chapter 2)

Prejudice. Derived from two word parts meaning "before" (*pre-*) and "judge" (*-judice*). When it comes to race, *prejudice* means you "judge before." You make preconceived judgments about people—both positive and negative—based on race. Prejudice often leads to **discrimination.** (Chapter 1)

Privilege (category **Power Audit**). An unearned advantage. (Chapter 10)

Prosperity (category **Power Audit**). Resources of time, talent, and treasure. Color-courageous disciples seek to steward a portion of their prosperity to foster biblical equity. (Chapter 10)

Pro-White Preference (category **Unconscious Bias**). Many people harbor a preference for Whiteness and a corresponding aversion to Blackness. Tragically, almost half of African Americans also harbor anti-Black bias themselves. (Chapter 4)

Race. A man-made system that divides humans into categories based on visible traits like skin color, usually so that one racial group might gain power over another group. (Chapter 1)

Racial Privilege. Most, if not all, societies harbor an invisible hierarchy in which some races, ethnicities, or cultures have historically held greater status than others. This invisible hierarchy confers unearned advantage to those racial groups at the top of the hierarchy. (Chapter 10)

Racial Profiling. The utilization of race as a grounds for suspected wrongdoing or criminal behavior. An example: Studies show that Black drivers are more likely to be pulled over than White drivers. (Chapter 4)

Racialized Society. A society in which race matters profoundly for differences in life experiences, life opportunities, and social relationships. If a society's systems persistently result in different outcomes for different races, you have a racialized society. (Chapter 3)

Racial Supremacy. The conscious or unconscious conviction that one race is the standard and/or is superior to others. Disciples are called to replace all forms of racial supremacy with the supremacy of Jesus Christ.

Racism. Personal racial prejudice *plus* systemic practices of institutions that lead to racial inequity in society. The shorthand for racism is Personal Prejudice + Systemic Inequity. (Chapter 1)

Reconciliation. The process of making broken things whole again. Since creation is broken on every level, it requires reconciliation on every level (individual, interpersonal, systemic, cosmic). God's plan is to reconcile all things to himself through Christ (Colossians 1:19–20). God also entrusts disciples with "the ministry of reconciliation" (see 2 Corinthians 5:17–21). (Chapter 2)

Rediscipleship. The idea that all people have to some extent been unconsciously "discipled" by the racial narratives of the world; this suggests the need to be discipled again. (Chapter 5)

Redlining. A once-legal discriminatory lending practice that limited mortgage financing opportunities for people of color. (Chapter 9)

Restitution. To restore something that was lost. (Chapter 7)

Reverse Racism. Refers to the alleged exchange of one unfair racial preference for another unfair racial preference. (Chapter 6)

Sankofa. *Sankofa* is a word from the Akan tribe in Ghana, derived from *san* (to return), *ko* (to go), and *fa* (to fetch, seek, and take). The Sankofa symbol is a bird reaching backward for nourishment. *Sankofa* means that we must look back before we can faithfully move forward together. (Chapter 9)

School-to-Prison Pipeline. Once Black children enter the criminal justice system, often beginning with minor school disciplinary measures, they are far more likely than White children to be sentenced again as adults. (Chapter 3)

Shalom. Often translated as "peace" in the Bible, shalom is the way things ought to be. It describes the experience of wholeness and flourishing in our relationships with God, with one another, and with all creation. (Chapter 1)

Shame. The intensely painful feeling that one is unworthy of love and belonging. (Chapter 5)

Sin. Any action that is contrary to God's design, including choosing our own will instead of God's will. The Bible says that "all have sinned and fall short of the glory of God" (Romans 3:23) and that the penalty of sin is death (Romans 6:23), which is why we need the Savior, Jesus Christ. (Chapter 2)

Solidarity. The experience of being united as one body in common life and purpose; a voluntary sharing of joys and challenges as an expression of unity. (Chapter 6)

Status Quo Bias (category **Unconscious Bias**). The human tendency to resist changes to the status quo, even when those changes are shown to be beneficial. (Chapter 4)

Stereotype Threat (category **Unconscious Bias**). A phenomenon in which a person's anxiety about confirming a negative stereotype leads to underperformance. (Chapter 4)

Systemic. Impacting not only individual people but entire systems as a whole. (Chapter 1)

Systemic Racism. Patterns of racial inequity that characterize systems, policies, and institutions as a whole. (Chapter 1)

Transgenerational Racial Trauma. Trauma that is passed down genetically. (Chapter 5)

Trauma. From the Greek for "wound," *trauma* describes the spiritual, emotional, and relational wounds that linger and continue to cause pain after a distressing event. (Chapter 5)

Truth Distortion (category **Unconscious Bias**). A category of unconscious bias that happens when the human mind distorts what is true. Examples include **Confirmation Bias,** the **Ostrich Effect,** and the **Bias Blind Spot.** (Chapter 4)

Unconscious Bias (or **Implicit Bias**). The biases we unconsciously hold that create a gap between our intentions and our impact when it comes to fair treatment and biblical equity. (Chapter 4)

Vicarious Trauma. The trauma that results when a person of color witnesses someone else's racial trauma either directly (firsthand) or indirectly (secondhand or thirdhand). (Chapter 5)

Voter Suppression. When some citizens make it harder for other citizens to vote. Examples include poll taxes, literacy tests, state laws, outright intimidation, and more. (Chapter 9)

White. Refers to those who are not people of color, particularly people of European descent. (Chapter 1)

White Supremacy. A type of **racial supremacy** that understands the White race to be the standard and/or superior to others.

Woke. Aware of and attentive to important social issues, particularly matters related to racial injustice. More recently, the term has taken on negative connotations, referring to extreme political correctness; this is a deviation from the term's original intent. (Chapter 3)

Zero-Sum Paradigm. The conviction that one racial group's gain comes at another group's loss. In reality, racial zero-sum thinking in America has led to the diminishment of life for everyone in nearly every sector, including education, housing, labor, public recreation, and the environment. (Chapter 6)

You're still early in the journey of life, and no doubt you are still working out the answers to *many* questions. Questions like:

- Why am I here?
- What is the purpose of my life?
- Is there a God? If so, why does God allow so much pain and suffering?
- Do I matter? Can I really make a difference?

If you've been paying any attention to the world, it's probably obvious to you that it is a pretty broken place. Racial inequity is *just one* of the many ways that the world is broken. And you're not the one who broke everything—it was pretty messed up by the time you arrived! Is there a God who sees all of this? If so, does he care? And if God does care, what is he doing about it?

The good news is this: God *does* see, and God *does* care. God loves the world, and God loves *you*. In fact, the Bible says that *God is love.* (How cool is that!) And do you know what love does? Love heals; love helps; love makes broken things whole again. Let's be clear about this: God didn't break the world either. Nope. The truth is this: *Our broken world breaks God's heart too.* That's why our God—who is love—is on a mission to make all the broken things of the world whole again. Making broken things whole again is called *reconciliation*. And get this: God invites *you* to join him on his reconciliation mission. It's the greatest adventure that one can experience in life.

If I had to summarize what's up with our broken world and how you can help make it whole again, I'd sum it up with these four ideas. (I included Bible verses in case you want to read more for yourself—which I highly recommend! Need help with that? Jump to the section at the end called "How to Look Up a Bible Verse.")

1. God exists, and God *is* love. God loves you and has a wonderful, loving purpose in mind for you, for your community, and for the whole world.
God is love—in fact, God has so much love that he created the whole universe from an overflow of love. That includes *you*. In fact, from the very beginning, God had you in mind. The Bible says that you are God's masterpiece and that he specifically designed you in his image. You are a one-of-a-kind creation, tailor-made to offer uniquely beautiful contributions to the world. What's more, God never intended you to be lonely or alone. God's design is for you to be part of a *beloved community*. God always intended humanity to be a diverse community of unique individuals, coming together in love as a united whole; every race, ethnicity, and culture part of a beautiful tapestry or mosaic work of art. *God's* stunning work of art. In the beginning, everything was good, perfect, beautiful, and whole on every level. (1 John 4:16; Ephesians 2:10, 14–15; Genesis 1:31; 2:18; Revelation 7:9)

2. But the whole world—and God's heart—was broken because of our sin. That's because the sad but natural result of sin is brokenness, pain, and death.

If God is so loving, then why is our world such a mess? The short answer is *sin.* Sin is anything we do that is contrary to God's design. Sin happens whenever we reject God or choose to do life apart from God. We weren't *designed* to do life apart from God—so eventually, the outcome of sin is always brokenness, pain, and death. The problem started when the very first humans sinned. But you know what? Every single one of us is guilty of sin. If we're honest, we have to admit that we each contribute to the brokenness of the world in different ways. Our sins may look different, of course. People sin in ways that are both large and obvious, but also in ways that are subtle and hidden to everyone but themselves. But we all sin. This is how the Bible puts it: "All of us . . . have left God's paths to follow our own" (Isaiah 53:6, NLT). And this explains why the world is broken on every level—in our personal lives, in our relationships (including racial prejudice), in our systems and organizations (including systemic racism), and even in creation itself. And all this brokenness that sin has caused also breaks God's heart. But here's the good news: God has done something about it! (Romans 3:23; 6:23; 8:19)

3. God loved the world so much that he sent his Son Jesus to save us. In fact, the name *Jesus* means "the Lord saves." When Jesus died for us on the cross and then rose again to new life, he defeated sin and death forever. He saved us and provided a beautiful way for us to become completely whole again.

If you want to understand God and God's love, all you have to do is look at Jesus. Why? Because Jesus was God's own Son, and his entire mission was to show us what God was like and make things whole again. He showed God's love by preaching good news, healing the sick, welcoming the marginalized, comforting the hurting, feeding the hungry, and teaching us how to love. Through it all, he lived a sinless life. But the most amazing way that Jesus showed God's love was by dying on the cross *for us*. The Bible describes it beautifully: "He was pierced for our rebellion, crushed for our sins. He was beaten so we could be whole. He was whipped so we could be healed" (Isaiah 53:5–6, NLT). Three days later, Jesus rose again from the dead, proving that he defeated sin and death forever. This is no ordinary love; it is the exquisite, outstanding, lavish love of God—a love powerful enough to make everything whole, including you. (John 3:16; Matthew 1:21; 4:23–25; 9:10–13; 2 Corinthians 5:21; 1 Peter 2:24; Isaiah 53:5–6; Luke 24)

4. God now invites you to be made whole so that you can be an agent of wholeness to the world. He offers to transform you so that you can join his mission to transform the world. Now God is inviting *you* to be transformed so that you can join him in transforming the world. The first step is to say yes to Jesus as *Savior* and as *Lord*. When you say yes to Jesus as *Savior*, it means that you agree with God that you have sinned and that you need God to save you from sin, brokenness, and death. When you say yes to Jesus as *Lord*, it means that you will allow him to be the leader of your life—that you will choose God's path instead of your own path; that you will follow Jesus every day and join a community of Christians (like a church or youth group), a beloved community that is following Jesus together. As you do, Jesus will show you how to live, love, and join his mission to restore healing and wholeness to the world—starting with *your* world. (Romans 10:9; Matthew 4:19; 28:19–20; Acts 1:8; Hebrews 10:25; 2 Peter 3:18)

If you would like to say yes to Jesus now, you can pray (talk to God) in your own words, or you can use these words as a guide:

God, thank you so much for loving me and the whole world enough to send your Son, Jesus, to die for us. I agree with you that I am a sinner and that I am broken, and I want to accept the free gift of wholeness and everlasting life that Jesus provides. Please help me to know and grow in your love, and empower me to bring your wholeness and love to the whole world. Amen.

If this book has helped you start a new journey with God, please let a pastor or a Christian friend know, and find out how you can join a church community of people that can help you take the next steps from here. I would also *love* to hear from you, congratulate you, and pray for you! You can find me at http://michelletsanchez.com. I'd love to hear your story.

HOW TO LOOK UP A BIBLE VERSE

Every Bible verse has three parts in order to help you find God's words: (1) the name of a *book* (listed in the Bible's table of contents), (2) the *chapter* (the large numbers throughout each book), and (3) the *verse* (the tiny numbers throughout each book).

Let's give it a try with *John 3:16*—which means the book of John, chapter 3, verse 16. Find a Bible and look for the book of John in the table of contents. (Look carefully, because the book of John is different from the book of "1 John," for example.) Once you go to the book of John, flip the pages until you find chapter 3 (the big number) and then within that chapter, verse 16. Although your Bible translation may say it a little differently, you should find something like this: *"For God so loved the world that he gave his one and only Son, that whoever believes in him shall not perish but have eternal life"* (NIV).

If you're just getting started, I recommend using a Bible translation that is written in today's language so that it will be easier to understand. Some translations that I like personally are the New Living Translation (NLT) and the New International Version (NIV).

If you want to purchase a new print Bible, one that I would recommend is called the *Life Application Study Bible*. You can find it pretty much anywhere Bibles are sold. This Bible includes lots of easy-to-understand explanations to help you better comprehend what you are reading. It's kind of like having a private Bible teacher—which would obviously be super helpful!

Of course, you can also download the YouVersion Bible app or go to www.biblegateway.com or a similar website to search any Bible verse you want. But nothing beats having your own Bible and knowing how to read it.

During our generation, we have experienced an extraordinary racial awakening—which means that you also have an extraordinary opportunity to engage your kids in racial discipleship.

Although your kids might spend a few hours each week at church or youth group, they will spend far more hours over the course of their lives with you. This means that *you* play the most vital role in discipling your kids. There is so much you can do as a parent to shape the next generation and make a difference.

No doubt, discipling your kids raises some questions, though! Here are some brief answers to questions you might have on the journey of discipling your kids around race.

WHY SHOULD I DISCIPLE MY KIDS AROUND RACE?

Kids should, of course, be discipled in traditional Christian doctrines and practices like Bible reading and prayer. But beyond this, kids need to be discipled toward a Christlike perspective in *every* area of life—especially those areas that we tend to shy away from, like money, sexuality, and race. Why? Because your kids are already being formed each and every day by something or someone else. If they are not being discipled by the church or by you, you can be sure that they are certainly being influenced, shaped, and "discipled" by the world and its values instead.

WHEN SHOULD I START TALKING
TO MY KIDS ABOUT RACE?

Early and often! Research has shown that even as early as preschool, kids use racial categories during playtime to identify, exclude, and even negotiate power with other kids. Ideally, you would start talking to your kids about race before they even fully realize that it's a "challenging" topic! But really: It's never too early, and it's never too late.

WHAT DO YOU MEAN BY
COLOR-COURAGEOUS DISCIPLESHIP?

Color-courageous discipleship is a lifelong journey characterized by following Jesus, dismantling racism, and building beloved community. All three are key: (1) *following Jesus*—understanding Jesus's heart for all people and following his example; (2) *dismantling racism*—learning to recognize both subtle and overt forms of racism and committing to undoing them; and (3) *building beloved community*—fostering communities of unity, diversity, and Christlike love.

WHY IS THE CONCEPT OF ANTIRACISM HELPFUL?

Perhaps you are thinking, *I don't really want to be anti-anything! That sounds so negative.* When it comes to the racism conversation, I must admit that there are no perfect words. Rather than the word *antiracism,* some prefer phrases like *racial righteousness* and *racial reconciliation.* These are good, and you should feel free to use them if you prefer. For me, the word *antiracism* has been most transformational. Aiming to be an "antiracist" disciple has made it crystal clear to me that being "nonracist" is not enough; that being "neutral" in matters of race is not sufficient. Racial inequity is a big problem—it's been with us for centuries, and it won't go away anytime soon unless we all start doing something very different. When it comes to defeating racism, the word *antiracism* clarifies for me that we need to be proactive and intentional in resisting racism if we hope to make a real and lasting difference.

WHAT IS MOST IMPORTANT IN DISCIPLING COLOR-COURAGEOUS KIDS?

Actually, what's most important as a parent is not what you *say* but what you *do*. Your kids will naturally reproduce your behavior. So the best way to disciple color-courageous or antiracist kids is to be a color-courageous disciple yourself. Get started on the journey if you haven't, and if you've been on the journey for a while, guard your heart against the conviction that you've "arrived." Your kids are far more likely to be transformed if they witness transformation in you.

HOW SHOULD I GO ABOUT IT?

When it comes to discipleship, I find it helpful to think in three categories: head, heart, and hands. (1) *Head:* How are you and your kids growing in awareness and knowledge of racial inequity, past and present? (2) *Heart:* How are you and your kids being mentored and shaped through multiethnic relationships and tangible experiences? (3) *Hands:* How are you and your kids taking concrete actions together to make a difference? All three—head, heart, and hands—are best engaged over the course of everyday life and as current events arise. As you look out for them, you will see that the possibilities are endless.

WHAT IF I MESS UP?

The question is not *what if* you mess up . . . but *what happens when you do!* You *will* make mistakes along the way because you're still on the journey too. And guess what? That's part of the learning process. In fact, I *encourage* you to share your mistakes and learnings with your kids. As you do, you will model humility, perseverance, and a growth mindset—all of which are critical to color-courageous discipleship. Rest assured: Your kids will probably learn more from what you do imperfectly than from what you do perfectly.

WHAT OTHER RESOURCES DO YOU RECOMMEND?

The good news is that new resources are constantly emerging. One Christian resource that I highly recommend is *How to Fight Racism* by Jemar Tisby, with editions for both adults and young people. In simple language, Tisby explains how to fight racism from a biblical perspective through the ARC of racial justice: awareness, relationships, and commitment.

A second excellent resource is *The Race-Wise Family: Ten Postures to Becoming Households of Healing and Hope* by Helen Lee and Michelle Ami Reyes.

A final resource is EmbraceRace (www.embracerace.org). Although it's not a Christian organization, I have deeply appreciated many of their resources. EmbraceRace was founded by two parents who set out to create a community and gather the resources needed to meet the challenges faced by those raising children in a world where race matters.

You can find more on my website at http://michelletsanchez .com. And if you have children, your family might enjoy my picture book *God's Beloved Community*. It's color-courageous discipleship in its simplest form and features gorgeous illustrations too.

May God be with you on your family's color-courageous discipleship journey!

NOTES

CHAPTER 1: INVITATION TO A RACIAL DISCIPLESHIP JOURNEY

1. David W. Swanson, *Rediscipling the White Church: From Cheap Diversity to True Solidarity* (Downers Grove, Ill.: IVP, 2020).

2. His fifth group, *Monstrosus,* applied to people with visible disabilities. See Tiffany Jewell, *This Book Is Anti-Racist* (Minneapolis: Frances Lincoln Children's Books, 2020), 154.

3. Erin N. Winkler, "Children Are Not Colorblind: How Young Children Learn Race," *PACE: Practical Approaches for Continuing Education* 3, no. 3 (2009): 1–8.

4. Sarah Mervosh, "How Much Wealthier Are White School Districts Than Nonwhite Ones? $23 Billion, Report Says," *The New York Times,* February 27, 2019, www.nytimes.com/2019/02/27/education/school-districts-funding-white-minorities.html.

5. *Lexico.com,* s.v. "adventure (*n.*)," www.lexico.com/en/definition/adventure.

6. *Merriam-Webster,* s.v. "courage (*n.*)," www.merriam-webster.com/dictionary/courage.

CHAPTER 2: A CHRIST-CENTERED APPROACH TO ANTIRACISM

1. Steven S. Skiena and Charles Ward, *Who's Bigger? Where Historical Figures Really Rank* (Cambridge: Cambridge University Press, 2014).

2. John S. C. Abbott, ed., *Confidential Correspondence of the Emperor Napoleon and the Empress Josephine* (New York: Mason Brothers, 1856), 359, 361. This additional reflection from Napoleon is noteworthy. He said that Christianity is "the only religion which destroys . . . prejudice, the only one which proclaims the unity and the absolute brotherhood of the whole human family." *Confidential Correspondence,* 360.

3. George A. Yancey, *Beyond Racial Gridlock: Embracing Mutual Responsibility* (Downers Grove, Ill.: IVP Books, 2006), Kindle.

4. I have long envisioned the multilayered reconciliation that our world needs as a series of concentric circles, and it seems that numerous other thinkers have embraced a similar vision. For example, Lisa Sharon Harper has portrayed circles that include self, gender, family, creation, governing structures, and nations in *The Very Good Gospel: How Everything Wrong Can Be Made Right* (Colorado Springs, Colo.: WaterBrook, 2016), 34. My friend Cheryl Lynn Cain, in a school paper, depicted these circles as personal, interpersonal, systemic, and all creation, with all things holding together in God. I also thank Cheryl for highlighting that the Christ-hymn of Colossians 1 is a beautiful *song* of reconciliation.

5. This is a poetic Scripture quote and paraphrase taken from Matthew 14:27; 28:20; and Revelation 22:13.

PART 2: COLOR-COURAGEOUS PARADIGM SHIFTS

1. Edward J. Blum and Paul Harvey, *The Color of Christ: The Son of God and the Saga of Race in America* (Chapel Hill: University of North Carolina Press, 2012), Kindle.

CHAPTER 3: DISCIPLESHIP AS AWAKENING

1. Josephine Sedgwick, "25-Year-Old Textbooks and Holes in the Ceiling: Inside America's Public Schools," *The New York Times,* April 16, 2018, www.nytimes.com/2018/04/16/reader-center/us-public-schools-conditions.html.

2. A must-read on this topic is Ken Wytsma, *The Myth of Equality: Uncovering the Roots of Injustice and Privilege* (Downers Grove, Ill.: IVP Books, 2017).

3. Christian Smith and Michael O. Emerson, *Divided by Faith: Evangelical Religion and the Problem of Race in America* (Oxford: Oxford University Press, 2000), 7.

4. This section is modeled on the outstanding and frequently updated Ben & Jerry's blog post, "7 Ways We Know Systemic Racism Is Real," Ben & Jerry's (blog), www.benjerry.com/whats-new/2016/systemic-racism-is-real.

5. Neil Bhutta, Andrew C. Chang, Lisa J. Dettling, and Joanne W. Hsu, "Disparities in Wealth by Race and Ethnicity in the 2019 Survey of Consumer Finances," Board of Governors of the Federal Reserve System, September 28, 2020, www.federalreserve.gov/econres/notes/feds-notes/disparities-in-wealth-by-race-and-ethnicity-in-the-2019-survey-of-consumer-finances-20200928.htm.

6. Jenna Ross, "The Racial Wealth Gap in America: Asset Types Held by Race," Visual Capitalist (blog), June 12, 2020, www.visualcapitalist.com/racial-wealth-gap.

7. Matt Bruenig, "The Top 10 Percent of White Families Own Almost Everything," *The American Prospect,* September 8, 2014, https://prospect.org/power/top-10-percent-white-families-almost-everything.

8. "The Racial Disparity in Homeownership Rates Persists," Joint Center for Housing Studies of Harvard University, www.jchs.harvard.edu/son-2020-homeownership-gap.

9. Gail Marksjarvis, "Why Black Homeownership Rates Lag Even as the Housing Market Recovers," *Chicago Tribune,* July 21, 2017, www.chicagotribune.com/business/ct-black-homeownership-plunges-0723-biz-20170720-story.html.

10. *The Future of Fair Housing: Report of the National Commission on Fair Housing and Equal Opportunity,* The National Commission on Fair Housing and Equal Opportunity, December 2008, 8, https://lawyerscommittee.org/wp-content/uploads/2015/08/The-Future-of-Fair-Housing-National-Commission-on-Fair-Housing-and-Equal-Opportunity.pdf.

11. See chart "Denial Rates for Home Loan Applications, by Race," in Shayanne Gal, Andy Kiersz, Michelle Mark, Ruobing Su, and Marguerite Ward, "26 Simple Charts to Show Friends and Family Who Aren't Convinced Racism Is Still a Problem in America," *Business Insider,* July 8, 2020, www.businessinsider.com/us-systemic-racism-in-charts-graphs-data-2020-6.

12. Drew DeSilver, "Black Unemployment Rate Is Consistently Twice That of Whites," Pew Research Center (blog), August 21, 2013, www.pewresearch.org/fact-tank/2013/08/21/through-good-times-and-bad-black-unemployment-is-consistently-double-that-of-whites.

13. Janell Ross and National Journal, "African-Americans with College Degrees Are Twice as Likely to Be Unemployed as Other Graduates," *The Atlantic,* May 27, 2014, www.theatlantic.com/politics/archive/2014/05/african-americans-with-college-degrees-are-twice-as-likely-to-be-unemployed-as-other-graduates/430971.

14. Robert Manduca, "How Rising U.S. Income Inequality Exacerbates Racial Economic Disparities," Equitable Growth (blog), Washington Center for Equitable Growth, August 23, 2018, www.equitablegrowth.org/how-rising-u-s-income-inequality-exacerbates-racial-economic-disparities.

15. Sarah Mervosh, "How Much Wealthier Are White School Districts Than Nonwhite Ones? $23 Billion, Report Says," *The New York Times,* February 27, 2019, www.nytimes.com/2019/02/27/education/school-districts -funding-white-minorities.html.

16. Rose French, "Study: White Students Favored over Blacks in Gifted Programs," *The Atlanta Journal-Constitution,* January 19, 2016, www.ajc.com /news/local-education/study-white-students-favored-over-blacks-gifted -programs/ns6XS6kgfW8falN1YSybUK. *Civil Rights Data Collection: Data Snapshot: School Discipline* (Washington, D.C.: U.S. Department of Education Office for Civil Rights, March 2014), www2.ed.gov/about/offices/list/ocr /docs/crdc-discipline-snapshot.pdf.

17. Phillip Atiba Goff et al., "The Essence of Innocence: Consequences of Dehumanizing Black Children," *Journal of Personality and Social Psychology* 106, no. 4 (2014): 526–45, https://doi.org/10.1037/a0035663.

18. Kim Farbota, "Black Crime Rates: What Happens When Numbers Aren't Neutral," *HuffPost,* September 2, 2016, www.huffpost.com/entry/black -crime-rates-your-st_b_8078586.

19. Jennifer L. Eberhardt, *Biased: Uncovering the Hidden Prejudice That Shapes What We See, Think, and Do* (New York: Viking, 2019), 129–31.

20. "Racial Bias in the Justice System," interview of Christina Swarns (director of the Innocence Project), Innocence Project, September 17, 2009, https:// innocenceproject.org/racial-bias-in-the-justice-system.

21. Farbota, "Black Crime Rates."

22. "Criminal Justice Fact Sheet," NAACP, May 24, 2021, https://naacp.org /resources/criminal-justice-fact-sheet.

23. "Introduction to COVID-19 Racial and Ethnic Health Disparities," Centers for Disease Control and Prevention, December 10, 2020, www.cdc.gov /coronavirus/2019-ncov/community/health-equity/racial-ethnic-disparities /index.html.

24. Christen Linke Young, "There Are Clear, Race-Based Inequalities in Health Insurance and Health Outcomes," Brookings (blog), February 19, 2020, www.brookings.edu/blog/usc-brookings-schaeffer-on-health-policy /2020/02/19/there-are-clear-race-based-inequalities-in-health-insurance -and-health-outcomes. Samantha Artiga et al., "Health Coverage by Race and Ethnicity, 2010–2019," KFF (blog), July 16, 2021, www.kff.org/racial -equity-and-health-policy/issue-brief/health-coverage-by-race-and -ethnicity.

25. Khiara M. Bridges, "Implicit Bias and Racial Disparities in Health Care," *Human Rights Magazine* 43, no. 3 (2018), www.americanbar.org/groups/crsj

/publications/human_rights_magazine_home/the-state-of-healthcare-in-the
-united-states/racial-disparities-in-health-care.

26. Dayna Bowen Matthew, Edward Rodrigue, and Richard V. Reeves, "Time
for Justice: Tackling Race Inequalities in Health and Housing," Brookings
(blog), October 19, 2016, www.brookings.edu/research/time-for-justice
-tackling-race-inequalities-in-health-and-housing.

27. Mathieu Rees, "Racism in Healthcare: What You Need to Know," Medical
News Today, September 16, 2020, www.medicalnewstoday.com/articles
/racism-in-healthcare.

28. Xingyu Zhang et al., "Trends of Racial/Ethnic Differences in Emergency
Department Care Outcomes Among Adults in the United States from 2005
to 2016," Frontiers in Medicine 7 (2020): 300, https://doi.org/10.3389/fmed
.2020.00300.

29. Austin Frakt, "Bad Medicine: The Harm That Comes from Racism," The
New York Times, July 8, 2020, www.nytimes.com/2020/01/13/upshot/bad
-medicine-the-harm-that-comes-from-racism.html.

30. Richie Zweigenhaft, "Fortune 500 CEOs, 2000–2020: Still Male, Still
White," The Society Pages, October 28, 2020, https://thesocietypages.org
/specials/fortune-500-ceos-2000-2020-still-male-still-white. Allana Akhtar,
"Corporate America Is Seeing a Spike in the Age of CEOs Being Hired—and
Yes, They're Overwhelmingly White Men," Business Insider, November 1,
2019, www.businessinsider.in/strategy/news/corporate-america-is-seeing-a
-spike-in-the-age-of-ceos-being-hired-and-yes-theyre-overwhelmingly
-white-men/articleshow/71856494.cms. Also, Gal et al., "26 Simple Charts."

31. Gal et al., "26 Simple Charts."

32. Aaron Zitner, "The U.S. Has Elected Only Two Black Governors. Why That
Might Change," The Wall Street Journal, September 1, 2020, www.wsj.com
/articles/black-candidates-are-now-winning-in-mostly-white-districts
-opening-path-to-higher-office-11598980352.

33. Denise Lu et al., "Faces of Power: 80% Are White, Even as U.S. Becomes
More Diverse," The New York Times, September 9, 2020, www.nytimes.com
/interactive/2020/09/09/us/powerful-people-race-us.html.

34. Nicholas Kristof, "We're No. 28! And Dropping!," The New York Times, September 9, 2020, www.nytimes.com/2020/09/09/opinion/united-states-social
-progress.html.

35. Merriam-Webster, s.v. "woke (adj.)," www.merriam-webster.com/dictionary
/woke.

36. "Stay Woke: The New Sense of 'Woke' is Gaining Popularity," Merriam-
Webster, www.merriam-webster.com/words-at-play/woke-meaning-origin.

37. Martin Luther King, Jr., *Where Do We Go from Here: Chaos or Community?* (Boston: Beacon Press, 2010), 181.

38. Jemar Tisby, *The Color of Compromise: The Truth About the American Church's Complicity in Racism* (Grand Rapids, Mich.: Zondervan, 2019), Kindle, emphasis added.

39. King, *Where Do We Go from Here,* 10.

40. Barry Beckham, *Garvey Lives!: A Play,* 1972.

41. *The NIV Exhaustive Bible Concordance,* 3rd ed. (Grand Rapids, Mich.: Zondervan, 2015).

CHAPTER 4: DISCIPLESHIP AS WARDROBE CHANGE

1. David W. Swanson, *Rediscipling the White Church: From Cheap Diversity to True Solidarity* (Downers Grove, Ill.: IVP, 2020).

2. John Powell and Rachel Godsil, "Implicit Bias Insights as Preconditions to Structural Change," *Poverty and Race Journal* 20, no. 5 (October 2011): 3, https://prrac.org/implicit-bias-insights-as-preconditions-to-structural-change-by-john-powell-rachel-godsil-sept-oct-2011-pr-issue.

3. David Edmonds, "Implicit Bias: Is Everyone Racist?," *BBC News Online Magazine,* June 5, 2017, www.bbc.com/news/magazine-40124781.

4. Rachel D. Godsil and Alexis McGill Johnson, *Transforming Perception: Black Men and Boys* (Perception Institute, March 2013), 8, http://perception.org/wp-content/uploads/2014/11/Transforming-Perception.pdf.

5. Dolly Chugh, Katherine L. Milkman, and Modupe Akinola, "Professors Are Prejudiced, Too," Opinion, *The New York Times,* May 9, 2014, www.nytimes.com/2014/05/11/opinion/sunday/professors-are-prejudiced-too.html.

6. Jacques-Philippe Leyens et al., "Psychological Essentialism and the Differential Attribution of Uniquely Human Emotions to Ingroups and Outgroups," *European Journal of Social Psychology* 31, no. 4 (July 2001): 395–411, https://doi.org/10.1002/ejsp.50. "People attribute more uniquely human characteristics to the ingroup than to the outgroup."

7. Jennifer L. Eberhardt, *Biased: Uncovering the Hidden Prejudice That Shapes What We See, Think, and Do* (New York: Viking, 2019), 149.

8. Eberhardt, *Biased,* 145.

9. Godsil and Johnson, *Transforming Perception,* 8.

10. See German Lopez, "A New Study Shows Even 5-Year-Olds Can't Escape Racism," *Vox,* June 29, 2017, www.vox.com/identities/2017/6/29/15893172/study-racism-innocence-black-girls; Phillip Atiba Goff, Matthew Christian Jackson, Brooke Allison Lewis Di Leone, Carmen Marie Culotta, and Natalie

Ann DiTomasso, "The Essence of Innocence: Consequences of Dehumanizing Black Children," *Journal of Personality and Social Psychology* 106, no. 4 (2014): 526–45, https://doi.org/10.1037/a0035663; "Black Boys Viewed as Older, Less Innocent Than Whites, Research Finds," American Psychological Association, 2014, www.apa.org/news/press/releases/2014/03/black-boys-older.

11. See, for example, Civil Rights Data Collection, *An Overview of Exclusionary Discipline Practices in Public Schools for the 2017–2018 School Year* (U.S. Department of Education, Office for Civil Rights, June 2021), https://ocrdata.ed.gov/assets/downloads/crdc-exclusionary-school-discipline.pdf. Also Godsil and Johnson, *Transforming Perception,* 10.

12. *Social Science Literature Review: Media Representation and Impact on the Lives of Black Men and Boys* (The Opportunity Agenda, October 2011), https://bit.ly/blackmenboys, 24.

13. "When They See Us: Improving the Media's Coverage of Black Men and Boys," The Opportunity Agenda, 2019, www.opportunityagenda.org/explore/resources-publications/when-they-see-us-media.

14. Steve Stroessner and Catherine Good, "Stereotype Threat: An Overview," Femmes et Mathématiques, https://femmes-et-maths.fr/wp-content/uploads/2021/01/stereotype_threat_overview.pdf.

15. Gordon Hodson, "System Justification: Why People Buy Into Social Inequality," *Psychology Today,* February 16, 2017, www.psychologytoday.com/us/blog/without-prejudice/201702/system-justification-why-people-buy-social-inequality, emphasis added.

16. "The Ostrich Effect: Why and How People Avoid Information," Effectiviology, https://effectiviology.com/ostrich-effect.

17. Eberhardt, *Biased,* 217. See also Philip J. Mazzocco, *The Psychology of Racial Colorblindness: A Critical Review* (New York: Palgrave Macmillan, 2017).

18. Mazzocco, *Psychology of Racial Colorblindness.*

19. I'm grateful for the inspiration provided for this idea by Mellody Hobson, "Color Blind or Color Brave?," TED conference, March 2014, www.ted.com/talks/mellody_hobson_color_blind_or_color_brave.

20. "Studies also show that people will act according to egalitarian values when conscious that race may affect their decision-making." Godsil and Johnson, *Transforming Perception,* 11. See also Lily Zheng, "Practice Reduces Prejudice," Stanford SPARQ, https://sparq.stanford.edu/solutions/practice-reduces-prejudice; Kerry Kawakami et al., "Just Say No (to Stereotyping): Effects of Training in the Negation of Stereotypic Associations on Stereotype Activation," *Journal of Personality and Social Psychology* 78, no. 5 (May 2000): 871–88, https://doi.apa.org/doi/10.1037/0022-3514.78.5.871.

CHAPTER 5: DISCIPLESHIP AS INNER HEALING

1. Michael Balsamo, "Hate Crimes in US Reach Highest Level in More Than a Decade," *AP News,* November 16, 2020, https://apnews.com/article/hate-crimes-rise-FBI-data-ebbcadca8458aba96575da905650120d.

2. "FBI Releases 2020 Hate Crime Statistics," United States Department of Justice, August 30, 2021, www.justice.gov/hatecrimes/hate-crime-statistics.

3. "Bullying Statistics: By the Numbers," PACER's National Bullying Prevention Center, November 2020, www.pacer.org/bullying/info/stats.asp.

4. "Bullying Statistics," PACER's National Bullying Prevention Center.

5. "When Black Death Goes Viral, It Can Trigger PTSD-like Trauma," PBS NewsHour, July 22, 2016, www.pbs.org/newshour/nation/black-pain-gone-viral-racism-graphic-videos-can-create-ptsd-like-trauma.

6. Nora Chavez, "Shouldering Grief: Validating Native American Historical Trauma," NM CARES Health Disparities Center, https://hsc.unm.edu/programs/nmcareshd/docs/story_heart.pdf.

7. Chavez, "Shouldering Grief."

8. Chavez, "Shouldering Grief."

9. Resmaa Menakem, *My Grandmother's Hands: Racialized Trauma and the Pathway to Mending Our Hearts and Bodies* (Las Vegas, Nev.: Central Recovery Press, 2017), 39–40.

10. Menakem, *My Grandmother's Hands,* 40.

11. Menakem, *My Grandmother's Hands,* 56.

12. Menakem, *My Grandmother's Hands,* 40–56.

13. Vann R. Newkirk II, "Trump's EPA Concludes Environmental Racism Is Real," *The Atlantic,* February 28, 2018, www.theatlantic.com/politics/archive/2018/02/the-trump-administration-finds-that-environmental-racism-is-real/554315.

14. Malcolm X and Alex Haley, *The Autobiography of Malcolm X: As Told to Alex Haley* (New York: Ballantine, 1999), 3. First published October 1965.

15. Malcolm X and Haley, *The Autobiography of Malcolm X,* 5–6.

16. Michael Beschloss, "How an Experiment with Dolls Helped Lead to School Integration," *The New York Times,* May 6, 2014, www.nytimes.com/2014/05/07/upshot/how-an-experiment-with-dolls-helped-lead-to-school-integration.html.

17. In her short 2005 documentary film *A Girl Like Me,* Kiri Davis replicated the doll test and showed that the majority (fifteen out of twenty-one) of Black

children continued to "choose the white dolls over the black, giving similar reasons as the original subjects, associating white with being pretty or good and black with ugly or bad." 4TruthAndJustice, "Kiri Davis: A Girl Like Me," 2007, YouTube video, 0:07:15, www.youtube.com/watch?v=z0BxFRu _SOw.

18. Rebecca Rangel Campón and Robert T. Carter, "The Appropriated Racial Oppression Scale: Development and Preliminary Validation," *Cultural Diversity & Ethnic Minority Psychology* 21, no. 4 (October 2015): 497–506, https:// doi.org/10.1037/cdp0000037; Dawne M. Mouzon and Jamila S. McLean, "Internalized Racism and Mental Health Among African-Americans, US-Born Caribbean Blacks, and Foreign-Born Caribbean Blacks," *Ethnicity & Health* 22, no. 1 (February 2017): 36–48, https://doi.org/10.1080/13557858 .2016.1196652.

19. You can find the Racial Slur Database at www.rsdb.org. Its snarky tagline: "Impress your friends with your vast knowledge of hate!"

20. The 2011 documentary *Dark Girls* (directed by D. Channsin Berry and Bill Duke) poignantly explores colorism.

21. Jennifer Hochschild and Vesla Weaver, "The Skin Color Paradox and the American Racial Order," *Social Forces* 86, no. 2 (2007): 643–70, https://doi .org/10.1093/sf/86.2.643.

22. Hochschild and Weaver, "The Skin Color Paradox."

23. Menakem, *My Grandmother's Hands,* 271.

24. Brené Brown, "Shame vs. Guilt," Brené Brown (blog), January 15, 2013, https://brenebrown.com/articles/2013/01/15/shame-v-guilt.

25. Dana Brownlee, "This Therapist's Message to White Men: Become an Agent of Change or a Victim of Progress," *Forbes,* May 12, 2021, www.forbes.com /sites/danabrownlee/2021/05/12/this-therapists-message-to-white-men -become-an-agent-of-change-or-a-victim-of-progress.

26. Brené Brown, *Rising Strong* (New York: Spiegel & Grau, 2015), xx.

27. Brown, *Rising Strong,* 39.

28. Brené Brown, *I Thought It Was Just Me (but It Isn't): Making the Journey from "What Will People Think?" to "I Am Enough."* (New York: Gotham Books, 2007), introduction, Kindle.

29. Henri J. M. Nouwen, *Life of the Beloved: Spiritual Living in a Secular World* (New York: Crossroad, 2002), 43–45.

30. Nouwen, *Life of the Beloved,* 30–33.

31. "What Is PTG?," Posttraumatic Growth Research Group (blog), University of North Carolina at Charlotte, January 16, 2013, https://ptgi.uncc.edu/what-is -ptg.

32. Shelley H. Carson, "From Tragedy to Art: Meaning-Making, Personal Narrative, and Life's Adversities," *Psychology Today,* June 18, 2010, www.psychologytoday.com/us/blog/life-art/201006/tragedy-art-meaning-making-personal-narrative-and-life-s-adversities.

33. Martin Luther King, Jr., *Strength to Love* (Boston: Beacon Press, 1981), 44–45.

34. Desmond Tutu, *No Future Without Forgiveness* (New York: Doubleday, 2000).

35. Tutu, *No Future Without Forgiveness.*

36. King, *Strength to Love,* 50.

CHAPTER 6: DISCIPLESHIP AS BELOVED COMMUNITY

1. "The King Philosophy—Nonviolence365," The King Center, https://thekingcenter.org/about-tkc/the-king-philosophy.

2. Ibram X. Kendi, *How to Be an Antiracist* (New York: One World, 2019), 230.

3. George Yancey, *Beyond Racial Gridlock: Embracing Mutual Responsibility* (Downers Grove, Ill.: InterVarsity Press, 2022), Kindle.

4. Yancey, *Beyond Racial Gridlock,* Kindle.

5. Yancey, *Beyond Racial Gridlock,* Kindle.

6. Martin Luther King, Jr., "Letter from Birmingham Jail," The Martin Luther King, Jr., Research and Education Institute, https://kinginstitute.stanford.edu/sites/mlk/files/letterfrombirmingham_wwcw_0.pdf.

7. Martin Luther King, Jr., *Stride Toward Freedom: The Montgomery Story,* with an introduction by Clayborne Carson, The King Legacy Series (Boston: Beacon Press, 2010), 127–28.

8. Heather C. McGhee, *The Sum of Us: What Racism Costs Everyone and How We Can Prosper Together* (New York: One World, 2021).

9. *The Sum of Us: What Racism Costs Everyone and How We Can Prosper Together,* One World book description, www.oneworldlit.com/books/the-sum-of-us-hc.

10. Jonathan M. Metzl, *Dying of Whiteness: How the Politics of Racial Resentment Is Killing America's Heartland* (New York: Basic Books, 2019).

11. Robin J. DiAngelo, *White Fragility: Why It's so Hard for White People to Talk About Racism* (Boston: Beacon Press, 2018), 67–68.

12. Arthur Boers, "What Henri Nouwen Found at Daybreak," *Christianity Today,* October 3, 1994, www.christianitytoday.com/ct/1994/october3/4tb028.html, emphasis added.

13. Lawrence Barriner II and Danielle Coates-Connor, "Using #the4thbox: Play and Political Imagination," Interaction Institute for Social Change,

June 23, 2016, https://interactioninstitute.org/using-the4thbox-play-and -political-imagination.

14. Martin Luther King, Jr., "Remaining Awake Through a Great Revolution," The Martin Luther King, Jr., Research and Education Institute, https:// kinginstitute.stanford.edu/king-papers/publications/knock-midnight -inspiration-great-sermons-reverend-martin-luther-king-jr-10. Delivered at the National Cathedral, Washington, D.C., on March 31, 1968, and entered into the *Congressional Record* on April 9, 1968, emphasis added. Dr. King was likely using sweeping language to illustrate a wider point. The United States Homestead Acts transferred more than 270 million acres of land to individuals in the decades following the Civil War. Black people were technically eligible to receive land under these acts, and some certainly did. Nevertheless, for a variety of reasons, Black homesteading recipients were the exception rather than the rule; in reality, "almost all" of the ultimate beneficiaries were White. "Indeed, the Homestead Acts excluded African Americans not in letter, but in practice—a template that the government would propagate for the next century and a half." Keri Leigh Merritt, "Land and the Roots of African-American Poverty," Aeon, March 11, 2016, https://aeon.co/ideas/land-and -the-roots-of-african-american-poverty. See also Larry Adelman, "Background Readings," *Race—The Power of an Illusion,* PBS, www.pbs.org/race /000_About/002_04-background-03-02.htm.

15. Mark L. Russell et al., *Routes & Radishes: And Other Things to Talk About at the Evangelical Crossroads* (Grand Rapids, Mich.: Zondervan, 2010), 128.

16. Russell et al., *Routes & Radishes,* 128–29, emphasis added.

PART 3: COLOR-COURAGEOUS SPIRITUAL PRACTICES

1. Emmanuel Katongole, "From Tower-Dwellers to Travelers," interview by Andy Crouch, *Christianity Today,* July 3, 2007, www.christianitytoday.com/ct /2007/july/9.34.html.

2. Rose Dowsett, *The Cape Town Commitment: A Confession of Faith and a Call to Action,* Study Edition (Peabody, Mass.: Hendrickson, 2012).

CHAPTER 7: READ (IN LIVING COLOR)

1. "Cape Town 2010: The Third Lausanne Congress on World Evangelization," Lausanne Movement, www.lausanne.org/cape-town-2010-the-third-lausanne -congress-on-world-evangelization.

2. Ernest R. Randolph Richards and Brandon J. O'Brien, *Misreading Scripture with Western Eyes: Removing Cultural Blinders to Better Understand the Bible* (Downers Grove, Ill.: IVP Books, 2012).

3. Christian Smith and Michael O. Emerson, *Divided by Faith: Evangelical Religion and the Problem of Race in America* (Oxford: Oxford University Press, 2000), 76.

4. "What Is an Evangelical?," National Association of Evangelicals, 2022, www .nae.net/what-is-an-evangelical.

5. Timothy Keller, "A Biblical Critique of Secular Justice and Critical Theory," *Life in the Gospel,* https://quarterly.gospelinlife.com/a-biblical-critique-of -secular-justice-and-critical-theory.

6. Greg Asimakoupoulos, "A Head of His Time: How One of the Most Recognizable Images of Jesus Came to Be," Covenant Companion, February 8, 2016, https://covchurch.org/2016/02/08/a-head-of-his-time.

7. Asimakoupoulos, "A Head of His Time."

8. Mark Rosen, "Much-Beloved, Much-Maligned 'Head of Christ' Has Graced Many Walls—and Now a Dallas Museum," *The Dallas Morning News,* July 14, 2018, www.dallasnews.com/arts-entertainment/visual-arts/2018/07/15/much -beloved-much-maligned-head-of-christ-has-graced-many-walls-and-now -a-dallas-museum.

9. Asimakoupoulos, "A Head of His Time."

10. Paul Robinson, "We Can't Cancel 'White Jesus,' but We Can Keep Telling Our Church's Story," Religion News Service, June 29, 2020, https://religion news.com/2020/06/29/we-cant-cancel-white-jesus-but-we-can-keep -telling-our-churchs-story.

11. Giles Wilson, "So What Colour Was Jesus?," October 27, 2004, *BBC News Online Magazine,* http://news.bbc.co.uk/2/hi/uk_news/magazine/3958241 .stm.

12. James H. Charlesworth, *The Historical Jesus: An Essential Guide* (Nashville: Abingdon Press, 2008), 72.

13. Emily McFarlan Miller, "How Jesus Became White—and Why It's Time to Cancel That," Religion News Service, June 24, 2020, https://religionnews .com/2020/06/24/how-jesus-became-white-and-why-its-time-to-cancel -that.

14. Randy Woodley, *Shalom and the Community of Creation: An Indigenous Vision* (Grand Rapids, Mich.: Eerdmans, 2012).

15. James H. Cone, *The Cross and the Lynching Tree* (Maryknoll, N.Y.: Orbis Books, 2011).

16. See Dominique DuBois Gilliard, *Rethinking Incarceration: Advocating for Justice That Restores* (Downers Grove, Ill.: InterVarsity Press, 2018).

17. For more on these inspiring prison ministry movements, see for example Jonathan Sprowl, "The Church Inside: A New Movement in America's Prisons," *Outreach Magazine,* July 31, 2019, https://outreachmagazine.com

/features/discipleship/44484-the-church-inside-a-new-movement-in -americas-prisons.html. Also Troy Rienstra, "Partners in the Gospel: The Church Behind Bars," *The Christian Century,* October 3, 2006, www .christiancentury.org/article/2006-10/partners-gospel.

18. Justo L. González, *Santa Biblia: The Bible Through Hispanic Eyes* (Nashville: Abingdon Press, 1996). Robert Chao Romero, *Brown Church: Five Centuries of Latina/o Social Justice, Theology, and Identity* (Downers Grove, Ill.: IVP Academic, an imprint of InterVarsity Press, 2020).

19. Jemar Tisby, among others, does a spectacular job of tracing the history of the White church's complicity with racism in America. See Jemar Tisby, *The Color of Compromise: The Truth About the American Church's Complicity in Racism* (Grand Rapids, Mich.: Zondervan, 2019).

20. William H. Frey, "The US Will Become 'Minority White' in 2045, Census Projects," Brookings (blog), March 14, 2018, www.brookings.edu/blog/the -avenue/2018/03/14/the-us-will-become-minority-white-in-2045-census -projects.

CHAPTER 8: PRAY (IN THE RAW)

1. Mark Vroegop, *Dark Clouds, Deep Mercy: Discovering the Grace of Lament* (Wheaton, Ill.: Crossway, 2019), 28.

2. Vroegop, *Dark Clouds, Deep Mercy.*

3. Philip Yancey, *Disappointment with God: Three Questions No One Asks Aloud* (Grand Rapids, Mich.: Zondervan, 2015), 237.

4. Soong-Chan Rah, *Prophetic Lament: A Call for Justice in Troubled Times,* Resonate Series (Downers Grove, Ill.: InterVarsity Press, 2015), 22.

5. Mark Vroegop, *Weep with Me: How Lament Opens a Door for Racial Reconciliation* (Wheaton, Ill.: Crossway, 2020).

CHAPTER 9: PILGRIMAGE (FOR PERSPECTIVE)

1. "Sankofa: A Journey Toward Racial Righteousness," The Evangelical Covenant Church, https://covchurch.org/justice/racial-righteousness/sankofa, emphasis added. The ECC has preferred the terms *racial righteousness* and *racial reconciliation.* "Racial Righteousness," Minnehaha Academy, 2020, www .minnehahaacademy.net/about/racial-righteousness#fs-panel-7127.

2. Leland Ryken, James C. Wilhoit, and Tremper Longman III, eds., *Dictionary of Biblical Imagery,* s.v. "Pilgrim, Pilgrimage" (Downers Grove, Ill.: InterVarsity Press, 2000).

3. Ryken, Wilhoit, and Longman, *Dictionary of Biblical Imagery,* "Pilgrim, Pilgrimage."

4. James Harpur, *The Pilgrim Journey: A History of Pilgrimage in the Western World* (Katonah, N.Y.: BlueBridge, 2016), 6.

5. Christian Timothy George, *Sacred Travels: Recovering the Ancient Practice of Pilgrimage* (Downers Grove, Ill.: InterVarsity Press, 2006), Kindle.

6. David P. Leong, *Race and Place: How Urban Geography Shapes the Journey to Reconciliation* (Downers Grove, Ill.: IVP Books, 2017), 56.

7. Leong, *Race and Place,* 41.

8. Tracy Hadden Loh, Christopher Coes, and Becca Buthe, "The Great Real Estate Reset: Separate and Unequal: Persistent Residential Segregation Is Sustaining Racial and Economic Injustice in the US," Brookings (blog), December 16, 2020, www.brookings.edu/essay/trend-1-separate-and-unequal -neighborhoods-are-sustaining-racial-and-economic-injustice-in-the-us.

9. Loh, Coes, and Buthe, "The Great Real Estate Reset."

10. "Celebrating 10 Years of the Sankofa Journey," Covenant Newswire Archive (blog), January 20, 2009, http://blogs.covchurch.org/newswire/2009/01/20 /6816.

11. "Celebrating 10 Years."

12. "Celebrating 10 Years," emphasis added.

13. "Celebrating 10 Years," emphasis added.

14. "Celebrating 10 Years."

15. You can learn more about Debbie Blue's inspiring story from Bob Smietana, "True Blue," *Covenant Companion,* May 6, 2015, https://covchurch.org/2015 /05/06/true-blue.

16. George, *Sacred Travels,* 26.

17. Harpur, *The Pilgrim Journey,* 16, emphasis added.

18. Ryken, Wilhoit, and Longman, *Dictionary of Biblical Imagery,* "Pilgrim, Pilgrimage."

19. The celebration and/or commemoration of Jewish holidays by Christians, while of course no longer required, is a richly creative way to deepen our Old Testament foundations—foundations that remain vital to our Christian faith. For an excellent family guide on this, see Robin Sampson and Linda Pierce, *A Family Guide to the Biblical Holidays: With Activities for All Ages* (Woodbridge, Va.: Heart of Wisdom, 2001).

20. "Relocation," Christian Community Development Association, 2022, https://ccda.org/about/philosophy/relocation.

21. Michelle Ferrigno Warren, *The Power of Proximity: Moving Beyond Awareness to Action* (Downers Grove, Ill.: IVP Books, 2017), 22.

22. Dominique DuBois Gilliard, "Rethinking Incarceration to Fight Concentration Camps with Dominique DuBois Gilliard," in *Hope & Hard Pills,* podcast,

September 28, 2019, 39:15–39:43, https://hope-hard-pills.simplecast.com /episodes/rethinking-incarceration-to-fight-concentration-camps-with -dominique-dubois-gilliard-ure7pT17.

23. Billy Graham, *Who's in Charge of a World that Suffers? Trusting God in Difficult Circumstances* (Nashville: W Publishing Group, 2021), 87.

24. Leong, *Race and Place,* 56–57.

25. Harpur, *The Pilgrim Journey,* 17.

CHAPTER 10: FAST (FOR REAL)

1. Jonathan Wilson-Hartgrove, Anne Graham Lotz, and Dallas Willard, "What Classic Spiritual Discipline Needs the Most Renewal Among American Christians?," *Christianity Today,* March 12, 2013, www.christianitytoday.com /ct/2013/march/what-classic-spiritual-discipline-needs-most-renewal -among.html.

2. David W. Swanson, *Rediscipling the White Church: From Cheap Diversity to True Solidarity* (Downers Grove, Ill.: InterVarsity Press, 2020).

3. *Hamilton: An American Musical,* music and lyrics by Lin-Manuel Miranda, 2015.

4. *Biblical Advocacy 101,* Christian Reformed Church, www.crcna.org/sites /default/files/36318_osj_advocacy_brochure_can_web.pdf, emphasis added.

5. Jemar Tisby, *How to Fight Racism: Courageous Christianity and the Journey Toward Racial Justice* (Grand Rapids, Mich.: Zondervan, 2021), 195.

6. C. S. Lewis, *Beyond Personality: The Christian Idea of God* (London: Centenary Press, 1944).

MICHELLE T. SANCHEZ serves as executive minister of Make and Deepen Disciples for the Evangelical Covenant Church, a multi-ethnic movement of nine hundred congregations throughout North America. Her team produces discipleship resources for all ages, including children and youth. Michelle went to seminary at Gordon-Conwell Theological Seminary and studied the life of Jesus at Jerusalem University College. She is a frequent conference speaker and a columnist with *Outreach* magazine. Michelle is the author of three books with WaterBrook: *Color-Courageous Discipleship, Color-Courageous Discipleship Student Edition,* and the picture book *God's Beloved Community.* Michelle has thoroughly enjoyed experiencing colorful cultures in thirty-five countries and territories around the world—and counting! She and her husband, Mickey, live with their children in the Chicago area.

Follow Michelle on Twitter @michtsanchez.

For bonus materials, inquiries, and additional resources on color-courageous discipleship, please visit: https://michelletsanchez.com.

Discover a Christ-centered approach to antiracism that empowers all ages to celebrate God's heart for diversity and racial equity and to build beloved community.

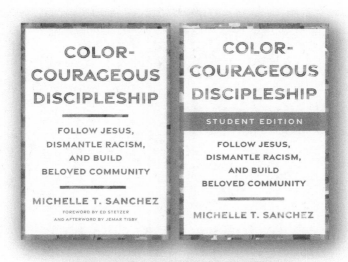